W9-BBH-571

FROM
THE TEMPLE TO
THE CASTLE

MATHEMATICA

MVSICA

ARCH. IL TTVRA

M.D.

XXXVI

GIANBA
TISTA

CON
IL SVO
OMENTO ET FIGVRE
VETRVVIO
IN VOLGAR LINGVA
RAPORTATO PER
M. GIANBATISTA
CAPORALI DI
PERVGIA

CAPORA
LI.

BENEFACIENTIBVS ABSTINE.

LITTERA
TVRA

PITTVRA

From the Temple to the Castle

An Architectural History of British Literature, 1660–1760 🦡

Lee Morrissey

UNIVERSITY PRESS OF VIRGINIA

Charlottesville and London

THE UNIVERSITY PRESS OF VIRGINIA
© 1999 by the Rector and Visitors of the University of Virginia
All rights reserved
Printed in the United States of America

First published 1999

⊗ The paper used in this publication meets the minimum requirements of the American National Standard for Information Sciences—Permanence of Paper for Printed Library Materials, ANSI Z39.48-1984.

Frontispiece: Title page of Caporali's edition of Vitruvius (1536). (Courtesy of Avery Architectural and Fine Arts Library, Columbia University in the City of New York)

Library of Congress Cataloging-in-Publication Data

Morrissey, Lee.
    From the temple to the castle : an architectural history of
British literature, 1660–1760 / Lee Morrissey.
        p.   cm.
    Includes bibliographical references and index.
    ISBN 0-8139-1899-5 (cloth alk. paper)
    1. English literature—18th century—History and criticism.
2. Architecture and liteerature—History—18th century. 3. English
literature—Early modern, 1500–1700—History and criticism.
4. Architecture and literature—History—17th century.
5. Aesthetics, Modern—18th century. 6. Aesthetics, Modern—17th
century. 7. Aesthetics, British. I. Title.
PR 448.A75M67   1998
820.9'357—dc21   98-50726
                                                      CIP

Finally, I would have the architect
take the same approach as one might
toward the study of letters.

—Leon Battista Alberti,

On the Art of Building in Ten Books 9.173

Contents

Illustrations

Acknowledgments

This study of literature and architecture, concerned with the degree to which literature can be considered one of the arts, has been profoundly affected by my experience in the College of Architecture, Arts, and Humanities at Clemson University. By supporting my courses on architectural theory and literary history, by involving me in the yearlong process of M.Arch. thesis committees, by enriching Clemson architectural education with a monthly lecture series by practicing architects, and by inviting me to participate in discussions about curricular change in architecture, my colleagues have, quite simply, improved this book. Thanks to their warm welcome, I have enjoyed an extraordinary, maybe even unique, interdepartmental opportunity to explore connections between literature and architecture. I thank James F. Barker, FAIA, Dean, and John Jacques, AIA, Director of the Graduate Architecture Program, for making this experience possible in such a friendly, respectful atmosphere.

My years as the Print Archivist for The Kitchen Center for Video, Music, Dance, Performance, Film and Literature, a contemporary arts center in Manhattan—during The Kitchen's involvement in the controversies of the so-called Culture Wars of the late 1980s and early 1990s, as it presented controversial artists (even as controversy flared up around them, in several cases)—taught me about the reality and complexity of the relationships between the arts and historical or social situations. It is difficult after that experience to imagine the arts as separated from the historical, although the same experience also taught me the importance of investigating how one imagines any connections between the arts and history. In conversations with staff and performers, as an audience member for Kitchen performances, and in compiling materials for *The Kitchen Turns 20*, my book on the history of The Kitchen, I was able to test the relevance of critical claims made about literature, the arts, artists, and, perhaps most importantly, the historical pressures on them. The controversies I witnessed at The Kitchen, like the differences of opinion among the authors discussed in this study, represent moments of cultural conflict and change, when something important is at issue in the arts—and in their ongoing definition. My sense of how artists might address historical circumstance in their art has been enriched by my experience there.

A project such as this one, in two fields and with five major authors, could not have reached this point without the help and advice of many individuals: Jim Basker, David Kastan, John Middendorf, Derek Moore, Franco Moretti, Michael Seidel, and Anders Stephanson, despite the many differences between their fields, each provided complementary guidance from the book's earliest stages. My thanks go to Tricia Thorpe, Steve Hull, Matthew Thorpe Hull, Liz Igoe, and Tony Clancy for patiently indulging my follies—or my photographing them, at least. Kevin Dettmar, Martin Jacobi, and the Clemson "Literary Theory Collective," by never taking for granted what literature is or what makes writing "literary," continually ask the provocative questions through which I have gained a greater understanding of my own arguments, and of what we talk about when we talk about literature. Susanna Schantz has read every word here—and quite a few that are no longer here—many times over. The best changes would not have happened without her.

Portions of this book have been previously published: chapter 4 appeared in a modified version in *The Age of Johnson: A Scholarly Annual* 9

(1998), and a version of chapter 5 appeared in *Questioning History: The Postmodern Turn to the Eighteenth Century*, a special issue of *Bucknell Review* 41:2 (1998): 86–99, edited by Greg Clingham. I thank both journals for their gracious permission to reprint my work here.

Introduction:
On Literature and Architecture

꿈 This study examines the relationship between literature and architecture in the works of a series of seventeenth- and eighteenth-century authors who were also architects—John Vanbrugh, Alexander Pope, and Horace Walpole—or whose writings demonstrate an abiding interest in architecture—John Milton and Thomas Gray. The study would seem on the face of it to be interdisciplinary, engaging the exchange of ideas between literature and architecture in these authors' careers. And, in ways that I address later in this chapter, it is interdisciplinary, of course. However, because the individuals under consideration were at least familiar with and in almost every case actually practicing in both literature and architecture, I did not have to bring together the two disciplines myself; I simply consider the author-architects' relationship to two fields that for them were already united, if only because they were interested in both. The individuals upon whom I focus made connections between literature and architecture; this book traces those connections. Thus, more than is typically the case, if in this book there are analogies between the arts, they are analogies made by the authors under consideration.

W. J. T. Mitchell has addressed this unique interdisciplinary predicament with reference to literature and the visual arts. Conceding the usual objections to interarts comparisons, he points out that "if one wants to see Blake's work for what it is, in short, one cannot avoid the problem of the image/text."[1] So too with figures such as Vanbrugh, the playwright who designed Blenheim Palace; Pope, the poet who offered architectural drawings redesigning friends' homes; or Walpole, the novelist who claimed that the home he renovated, Strawberry Hill, "was the scene that inspired" his novel *The Castle of Otranto*: if one wants to see their work for what it is, in short, one cannot avoid the problem of the architecture/text.[2] Because different opportunities for what would now be considered cross-disciplinary interaction obtained during the seventeenth and eighteenth centuries, this book should, on one level, be seen as a study in historical literary criticism, not interdisciplinary per se but attuned to different conditions of literary production. The careers of these author-architects invite us to reexamine distinctions usually made about literature, architecture, and history.

Taking its cue from the interests of these eighteenth-century British author-architects, this study reads architectural references made by them and architectural publications familiar to them and considers their literary works in architectural terms. It could be described as an intellectual history of late seventeenth- and eighteenth-century Britain, a history inflected by politics, using the materials of cultural history, considered in architectural terms. As a literary study of eighteenth-century British architectural theory and an architectural study of eighteenth-century British literature, this book represents an "architectural history" of British literature from 1660 to 1760. The chapters share a similar structure: first establishing a connection with architecture and the contemporary architectural moment in the careers of John Milton, Sir John Vanbrugh, Alexander Pope, Thomas Gray, and Horace Walpole and then describing how a principal text—*Paradise Lost, The Provok'd Wife, Essay on Man,*

"Elegy Written in a Country Churchyard," and *The Castle of Otranto*—focuses literary and historical issues in architectural terms. Although each chapter thus represents a distinct case history of each author-architect, the chapters are set in a narrative, a story of cultural change between 1660 and 1760, which reads their literary work for architectural references to show how what is called form responds to historical pressures (and, consequently, how formal responses might themselves change).

In the 1990s, as architecture has been embroiled in an argument over the nature and definition of architectural instruction, sociologist Robert Gutman is prompted to argue that "we are on the brink of a *fundamental transformation* of the basic structure of architectural education, as meaningful in its way as the inauguration of university schools of architecture 130 years ago."[3] The November 1991 edition of the *Journal of Architectural Education*, for example, published by the Association of Collegiate Schools of Architecture, focused on what the editors called "Postmodernizing Pedagogy." Similarly, in September 1995, to celebrate the appointment of Jorge Silvetti as the new chairman of the Department of Architecture, Harvard's Graduate School of Design hosted a series of talks on new directions in teaching and practice. Perhaps most visible in this recent reconsideration is the Carnegie Foundation report on architectural education, *Building Community: A New Future for Architecture Education and Practice*, by Ernest L. Boyer and Lee D. Mitgang, which argues that "making the connections, both *within* the architecture curriculum and *between* architecture and other disciplines on campus, is, we believe, the single most important challenge confronting architectural programs."[4] Originating for a variety of reasons—including the question of architecture's legibility, raised most visibly by Postmodern, New Urban, and Deconstructive approaches to architecture, not to mention the development of computer-aided design technologies—this process of making connections involves both reimagining architecture as an academic discipline and considering the nature of its emerging connections to the rest of the university. To some extent it is this latter possibility of cross-disciplinary institutional connections that the author-architects under consideration here offer to contemporary architectural education.

For upon visiting Britain in the mid–eighteenth century, André Rouquet wrote that "in England more than in any other country, every man would fain be his own architect"; the popularity of architecture in Britain was one of the most noticeable facets of "the present state of the arts in England."[5] During the eighteenth century, more than at any time preceding it, a combination of material factors helped to create this over-arching interest in architecture. There were, for example, demographic changes unique to the eighteenth century: between 1700 and 1800 England's population nearly doubled, rising from 5.4 to 9.2 million, and as might be expected, the relative urbanization of England also increased. Although only 5.8 percent of the early seventeenth-century British population lived in cities of 10,000 or more inhabitants, by 1650 that figure had grown to 8.8 percent; between 1650 and 1750 the percentage of the English population living in cities with at least 10,000 fellow citizens almost doubled again, to 16.7 percent.[6] At the same time, London, as the single most populated urban center in the Isles, contained 7.7 percent of the English population around 1650, a percentage which grew to 11.7 percent in 1750. In the eighteenth century only Constantinople, Peking, and Edo were bigger than London. In 1500 London's population "equaled that of the six largest provincial towns put together; by 1680 it exceeded the *sixty* largest."[7] In the nineteenth century, by contrast, London's population, as a percentage of the total English population, declined.

Besides these demographic changes and the pressures they placed on British architecture, Britain underwent several other spatial changes, with important symbolic resonances. The 1666 Fire of London (which destroyed four-fifths of the city in three days) and the subsequent fifty-year project of rebuilding, symbolized most visibly in the slow evolution and completion of Wren's St. Paul's Cathedral, prompted a reconsideration of the country's urban fabric.[8] The mid-eighteenth-century development of Bath and the rise of domestic tourism participated in a reevaluation of the relationship between Britain and its past and between London and the countryside. Finally, over the course of the century, the parliamentary Enclosure Acts reworked the British countryside more systematically than any preceding time, helping to prompt questions in the later eighteenth century concerning what was authentically British. Between 1760 and 1800 alone, there were "no fewer than 1,479 enclosure acts . . . dealing with rather more than four million acres of open fields," 10 percent of England as a whole.[9]

In seventeenth- and eighteenth-century Britain, becoming an architect did not require anything like the kind of professional training now associated with it. Until the second half of the eighteenth century, John Wilton-Ely points out, "the architectural scene was characterized by the continuing importance of the gentlemen architect."[10] M. S. Briggs is much more blunt: "Architectural education in the eighteenth century was almost non-existent."[11] According to James Ackerman, "The essential prerequisite for the practice of architecture was knowledge of Roman remains . . . gained . . . not only in Rome itself, but throughout Italy."[12] Someone traveling as part of their education could acquire all that was needed to be considered an architect, making it relatively easy, compared to a program of technical training and apprenticeship, which helps to explain how John Vanbrugh, Alexander Pope, and Horace Walpole could so easily practice. It may be that Swift was essentially right when he said, albeit disparagingly, of Vanbrugh: "*Van's Genius*, without Thought or Lecture, / Is hugely turn'd on *Architecture*," but his point could have applied to other architects as well.[13] Not even the greatest architect of the period, Sir Christopher Wren, was trained specifically as an architect; he had been a professor of mathematics before his first commission.

That architecture was an interest of the British reader as it had never been before is indicated by a boom in British architectural publications.

Between 1556 and 1700 only fifty-six new architectural titles were published in England—only one new book every three years.[14] Geoffrey Richards's 1663 translation of Palladio refers to "the scarcity of Books of architecture in English."[15] Not only was the output slow, but as Hanno-Walter Kruft puts it, "few works of any significance appeared in England in the seventeenth century."[16] In the eighteenth century, however, all that changed: "The eighteenth century was a Golden Age of architectural publications," according to Wilton-Ely.[17] Fifty-six new architectural titles were published during just the first three decades of the eighteenth century; where it had previously taken an average of three years for one title to appear, the early eighteenth century saw two new architecture books every year. The first third of the eighteenth century saw such important works as Colen Campbell's *Vitruvius Britannicus*, James Gibbs's *Book of Architecture*, so influential in the American colonies, and Robert Morris's theoretical treatise *Essay in Defense of Ancient Architecture*. It is with reference to such works that Kruft has argued that "although . . . England's contribution to architectural theory dates only from the beginning of the eighteenth century, it immediately acquired a position of virtual dominance in Europe."[18]

These publications, however, do more than simply indicate an architectural audience. As what Dora Wiebenson calls "documents of social change" in eighteenth-century Britain, they are an important resource; as a concise record of cultural change, they are invaluable. In a way that is not possible with buildings, architectural publications offer architects the chance to articulate the political and/or social reasons behind their formal, technical, and symbolic choices. In those writings architects and architectural theorists verbally articulate their built arguments. Because, as architect Bernard Tschumi argued, "the history of architecture is as much the history of its writings as of its buildings,"[19] joining those publications to the architectural interests of author-architects provides an even greater measure of change than the buildings themselves.

The disadvantages of taking eighteenth-century England as a literal model for late twentieth-century architectural education would seem clear: the many changes in materials alone require more technical training than any of these architects had; consequently, architecture today is a professional practice, one for which reinvestigating eighteenth-century architectural history and theory could seem ancillary at best. But the interest in architecture shared by the authors under consideration here familiarizes them with the way form, both literary and architectural, can negotiate a relationship between the arts and the historical. Architecture, littered as it is with different "languages of architecture" theories—the most recent one probably being deconstruction—has reason to distrust another seemingly similar approach. In general, it seems that architects are concerned that linguistic approaches to architecture would separate architecture from what is thought to be its most important Modernist legacy, articulated most famously by Le Corbusier: "It is a question of building which is at the root of the social unrest of to-day."[20] The concern is that considering architecture in literary terms means a loss of architecture's social commitments. The editors of *Reconstructing Architecture*, for example, believe that the shift "from a pursuit of architecture as a material agent of social change to an exploration of architecture as a language" has been "characterized as a disengagement from the modernist commitment to advance progressive projects."[21] Although linguistic theories of architecture may contain an element of this retreat from social change, it is not clear, on the one hand, that all nonlinguistic theories of architecture are thus by definition agents for social equality, nor, on the other, is it certain that such a retreat is a consequence of linguistic approaches.

For example, although it might seem that the social conditions of education in seventeenth- and eighteenth-century Britain would significantly limit the number of people who could become architects, in fact Barrington Kaye's analysis of the entries for architects in the *Dictionary of*

National Biography yields the surprising conclusion that the numbers and percentages of architects coming from the upper classes increased after 1789. Before 1789, according to Kaye, 41 percent of the architects came from "middle" and "working" classes, with only 9 percent from the upper classes. By 1850, 16 percent came from the upper class, 51 percent from the middle class, and only 2 percent from the working class. These figures suggest that, despite what we might have expected, the eighteenth century's flexible understanding of architecture played itself out in relatively flexible social access to architecture as a profession or as a practice.[22]

At the same time, there is a fear among architectural educators that, as Robert Beckley, architecture dean at the University of Michigan, contends, "for the proponents of the disciplinary approach, architecture is a language, with its own vocabulary, grammar, syntax, and history. It is pure and can be taught independent of political and social context. Architecture is timeless."[23] This book, however, argues that architecture can be a language and still participate in political and social contexts. In fact, the timelessness presumed to be implicit in focusing on the Palladian or neoclassical architecture of the late seventeenth and eighteenth centuries—with its classical allusions and its great houses, which today conventionally signify timeless stability—is an advantage in considering this period: if even the purest, most universal, and most timeless form of English architecture participates in, responds to, and affects political and social circumstances, then the same could be true for other periods and types of architecture as well.

Given architecture's concern about the ahistorical quality of linguistic theories of architecture, it is worth emphasizing that language is as social and as political as architecture, if not more so. Consequently, literature is not separate from the social, the political, or the historical. It is not, for instance, a mechanism for the unmediated transmission or reflexive transference of immutable values, what architect Thomas A. Dutton refers to as the "'literary-moral' definitions of culture."[24] Texts are as much products of their times as anything else (which is to say, of course, they are not entirely products of their times, either). Nor are texts literary only in the sense assumed by Françoise Choay's recently translated important comparison of literature and architecture, *The Rule and the Model: On the Theory of Architecture and Urbanism*, which not only "refrain[s] from interpreting architectural treatises, utopias, and urbanistic writings in terms of the cultural, economic, or political conditions in which they arose" but also attempts to "demonstrate their coherence."[25] For Choay, this coherence is to be taken as the marker of a literariness which itself shows how the text is removed from the conditions out of which it arose.

Literature and architecture are here both understood as types of purposeful metaphor, a larger rendering of the process of positing connections between unlike things, or perhaps a type of purposeful metonymy, a larger rendering of the process of ascribing a variety of different names to things (or, conversely, the same names to different things). In literature, it is because of this purposeful alternation between similarity and difference that a text can be both a product of its time and something that seems to transcend it; this alternation between metaphor and metonymy, between the apparently fictional (the metaphor) and the seemingly real (the name of the thing), modulates a text between one context and another. However, although it has what is probably the most important historic connection to the question of metaphor, literature is not the only field with a logical connection to metaphor. For metaphor, defined by architect Kenneth Frampton as "a human process by which we understand and structure one domain of experience in terms of another," is by no means an exclusively literary process.[26] Simply put, "metaphor and metonymy are ways of thinking analogously," writes Yuri Lotman, and thinking analogously happens in every field, including architecture.[27] As Kojin Karatani's recent book *Architecture as Metaphor* suggests, metaphor is as architectural as it is literary.

As purposeful metaphors (or metonymies), literature and architecture are here understood as rhetoric. In *Signs Taken for Wonders* (1983), Franco Moretti succinctly defines literary texts as "*historical* products organized according to *rhetorical* criteria."[28] The same definition could apply to a building—a historical construction organized according to rhetorical criteria—and, in some sense, such a definition has already been developed for it. Karsten Harries, for example, reworks Pevsner's claim that, as Harries writes, "the work of architecture is essentially a functional building with an added aesthetic component."[29] I have called that "aesthetic component" metaphor or rhetoric; architecture is building with metaphor. Similarly, Peter Eisenman argues that "the distinction between building and architecture depends on 'a sign of architecture.'"[30] In other words, on one level the distinction between building and architecture depends on a metaphor, a "sign." However, on another level it could be said that architecture is the rhetoric of building, meaning both that the difference between a mere building and successful architecture is rhetorical, and that architecture, as a study, has become the preferred discourse of building.

Although literature is made of words, for better or worse, we rarely actually think so; we tend to forget that literature is just words, and we become involved in, say, the meaning, or the form, or the argument, etc. This forgetting is understandable; believing that words have meaning (i.e., are anything other than the words) is the first suspension of disbelief. In fact, however, anytime one sees more than a word, one has fallen for the metaphor or the metonymy. And the same is true for architecture. At root, of course, architecture is made of building materials, in the same way that literature is made of words. Anytime one sees more than building materials arranged to provide shelter or to shape a space, one is falling for the metaphor or the metonymy. Diane Ghirardo, executive editor of the *Journal of Architectural Education*, has written about what she calls an "Architecture of Deceit"; I like the phrase but am afraid it is like the notion of figurative language, in making a distinction where there need not be any. In the same way that all language is figurative, all architecture is an architecture of deceit.

It is through metaphor, or metonymy, that what J. Mordaunt Crook in *The Dilemma of Style* calls "stylistic choices" act "as triggers to the imagination."[31] This stylistic dilemma involves the larger question of "how buildings mean," to quote the title of an essay by Nelson Goodman, who reminds us that "architectural works do not denote—that is, do not describe, recount, depict, or portray" and who argues that "they mean, if at all, in other ways."[32] I would say that architecture means metaphorically or metonymically. What Philip Johnson believes concerning art generally could apply to literature or architecture, understood as forms of metaphor: "Art is artifice, the opposite of truth: it's invention, it's lying, it's cheating the eye, it's subverting the psyche."[33] Although architecture deceives in many ways, including the structural impression of permanence or the seeming lightness of heavy materials, my own interest here, given the differences between the various author-architects under consideration, is in the stylistic deceits. Stylistic choices are here considered as rhetorical gestures, although it is true that understanding them in that way locates this argument (and, as I discuss in the Coda, it is an approach made possible by, and after, Walpole).

To say that the art side of architecture's combination of service and art is rhetoric may seem to imply that the social element of architecture is not real, i.e., that it is merely rhetorical. But as the art of persuasion, and sometimes as what Philip Johnson would call the art of deceiving, rhetoric is intrinsically social; it depends, for instance, on knowing your audience. Saying that literature or architecture is rhetorical does not mean that either of them is somehow separate from social or political situations; instead, it affects how one imagines connections between the aesthetic and the historical. For Kenneth Burke, and for this book, "critical and imaginative works are answers to questions posed by the situations in which they arose," with the important proviso that, as Burke adds, "the situations are real."[34]

If at first glance these authors seem to represent some predesignated architectural period type (from Renaissance to neoclassical or from baroque to Gothic, etc.), it is more important to ascertain why that form, or more specifically, why that rhetoric, best addressed the historical situation. Because rhetoric is here seen as a strategic response to a real situation, the relationship between literature or architecture and history is dialectical, not expressive. I am sympathetic to Lukács's claim that "every form is a resolution of a fundamental dissonance of existence," but I would qualify it by saying that although every form attempts to resolve or posits the resolution of a conflict, it is more likely that a "text does not resolve the conflict, it *names* it."[35]

In this sense, form is the rhetoric of representing a historical situation; moreover, it is precisely because form is rhetorical that it can be "apprehended as content" or that there can be a "content of the form."[36] Both form and content are rhetorical. However, there is a difference between form and rhetoric; there is a different rhetoric implied by the word *form*. Although it is often used as a substitute for meanings as different as story, text, and structure, such usage neglects the most important aspect of form, and of the rhetoric of form: shape, which entails space or spatial relations. Because "architecture is a shape in space and shapes space,"[37] because architects and architecture create forms, one of the advantages in considering literature and architecture rhetorically is that such consideration emphasizes the spatial quality of literary form or the rhetorical quality of architectural form.

Focusing on, correlating, and considering rhetorically literature and architecture in the careers of seventeenth- and eighteenth-century British authors over a one-hundred-year period accentuates the historical aspect of formalism and the formal aspects of historicism. That is, although the readings here rely on elements of formalism, with its attention to structuring devices, because the texts and authors considered have a connection with architecture, with shaping space, the focus on formalism already implies a notion of history. Or to consider it in the other direction, the narrative in this book relies on a notion of historical change and causal relations characteristic of historical study; but insofar as the literature studied has a connection with architecture, a spatial art, this historicism already entails a kind of formalism. More than being interdisciplinary or interarts, literature and architecture bridge the gap between today's historicist and formalist critical techniques and positions, exploring the relationship between literature and architecture to develop what might be called a historical formalism.

Fredric Jameson argues that "the political relationship of works of art to the societies they reside in can be determined according to the difference between replication (reproduction of the logic of that society) and opposition (the attempt to establish the elements of a Utopian space radically different from the one in which we reside)."[38] The relationship between a work and its time is a dialectical interplay between the rhetoric of resolution and the problem that form is supposed to resolve. What Jameson calls the difference between replication, making more of the same, and opposition, offering some alternative, can be seen in Robert Morris's *An Essay in Defense of Ancient Architecture* (1728), in which Morris contends that "the Decay of the State and Government of a Kingdom, is dependent upon the Decay of publick Buildings."[39] Morris clearly joins architecture and politics, making bad government dependent upon bad architecture. But the image of decay is perhaps more important for illustrating a rhetorical consideration of architectural form. Presumably decaying buildings would look uneven, jagged, or unfinished (as chapters 4 and 5 demonstrate, there was an interest in such buildings later in the eighteenth century), and Morris's interest in some alternative (probably smooth, even, symmetrical, and finished) implies that the symmetrical, orderly, standardized, and relatively easily propagated British neo-Palladian architecture best addressed what Morris considered to be the problem of political decay facing early eighteenth-century (i.e., post- seventeenth-century) Britain. Because it is not intrinsically clear that government in the abstract in the 1720s was better or worse than government at any other time, the Palladian alternative to political decay, which would seem to be a formal concern, should instead be seen as a rhetorical strategy.

Morris's argument is consistent with how architecture was self-consciously enlisted in a nationalist program—or, more accurately, in a series of nationalist programs—between 1660 and 1760. At the beginning of the period, for example, John Evelyn interrupts his 1664 translation of Fréart's *Parallel* to ask that "*Printers, Painters, Sculptors, Architects, &c.* . . . improve the Nation." Although his terms are architectural, one cannot help but assume that Evelyn is making a political, post–Civil War argument when he says that "it is often from the *assymetrie* of our Buildings, want of *decorum* and proportion in our Houses, that the irregularity of humours and affections may be shrewdly discern'd." That is, the civil war showed a lack of decorum, motivated by the disproportions and irregularities of the political houses—both the different, warring families and the political entities such as Parliament. Evelyn hopes that through "His Majesties great *Genius* . . . [they] may hope to see it all reform'd."[40] By "all" it seems that Evelyn meant politics as much as the arts; both the king and the king's patronage of the arts held out the possibility of reformation, political and cultural.

Having occurred so soon after the political Restoration, the Fire of London was taken as yet another possibility for nationalist reformation and improvement: a second Restoration. Dryden, for example, contends, in "Annus Mirabilis," that "since it was prophan'd by Civil War, Heav'n thought it fit to have it purg'd by fire" (1667, st. 276). Similarly, in the revised introduction to his translation of the first book of Palladio (1668, first edition 1663), Geoffrey Richards argues that "the re-building of London" constitutes "a second happy restoration, inferior only to that of his Majesties Person and Government." He joins the architectural and the political not only in his argument but also in his implicit assumptions about the design of the new buildings. Architecturally (or literally) his wish to avoid "that deformity and danger which we have formerly been liable to" could mean the London building practices that added a new story the previous one, until buildings jutted out over the streets and their roofs touched, turning streets into tunnels, and facilitating an easy exchange of fire. Politically, however, Richards is referring to the "danger" consequent upon the "deformity" of a government in civil war. Richards reminds his readers that "now . . . a new and great city is to be built," but this rebuilding could mean both that of the actual city of London, decimated by fire, and also that of the larger "polis" of England, which needs to be rebuilt after the civil war.[41]

Such seemingly extra-architectural implications permeate seventeenth- and eighteenth-century architectural publications, in part because in those centuries "what linked these texts across different disciplines, genres, styles, and periods was a relationship with building that could not be adequately described as figural."[42] But these implications are also there because of the connections between metaphor, rhetoric, and form that pervade literature and architecture generally, although all the more so during a period when architecture was extraordinarily popular and relatively accessible. Consequently, reading the literature and the architecture of these author-architects together provides a uniquely sensitive gauge of the rhetoric of cultural change during the late seventeenth and eighteenth centuries. As there is always more than one form in any historical period, and there are always variations within putative historical forms, the question then becomes why one text has one rhetoric or one form rather than another, a question which the careers of these author-architects are uniquely qualified to address.

"Truth . . . Is a Just and Naturall Proportion": Milton, Wotton, and Renaissance Architectural Theory

I

ᒼ⧽"IN POETRY, AS IN ARCHITECTURE, not only the whole, but the principal Members, and every part of them, should be Great."[1] So writes Joseph Addison in a 1712 *Spectator* essay whose initial formulation—"In Poetry, as in Architecture"—encapsulates the assumptions about literature and architecture that governed the seventeenth and eighteenth centuries and are under consideration in this book. For Addison, this comparison was an aside, an offhand comment, just a way of introducing his main point about the relationship between the parts of *Paradise Lost*. But the very fact that it was an aside suggests that it could then be assumed, that it was not a point that Addison needed to explain. Moreover, although Addison's claim sounds similar to that of a few recent architectural theorists who argue that architecture is like literature, recent criticism essentially reverses Addison's terms, contending not that "poetry is like architecture" but rather that "architecture is like poetry." Rather than the "language of architecture," Addison's point has more to do with how an architectural language can describe poetic structure, or already does.

Addison contends, for example, that although it "falls short of the

Aeneid or *Iliad*," as "a Poem in English" *Paradise Lost* is "like a stately Palace built of brick," with "Architecture in as great a Perfection as in one of Marble, tho' the Materials are of a coarser nature."[2] Addison's point, that the "the Materials" are less important than the "Architecture," probably applies to classical architectural theory generally: the form is more important than the materials. But the fact that Addison should be so specific as to tie *Paradise Lost* to a particular building material—brick—is also important; besides indicating a way of considering *Paradise Lost* architecturally, it also locates the poem in the context of typically seventeenth-century architectural issues. In what Timothy Mowl and Brian Earnshaw have recently described as "Puritan Minimalism," brick, "the new medium," was after 1660 "the fashionable building material," in part because it was relatively inexpensive.[3]

Like Addison, this chapter also understands Milton's poem in terms of seventeenth-century architecture, focusing principally on his references to Vitruvius, Alberti, and Sir Henry Wotton, whose key terms can be seen in Milton's prose pamphlets, such as *The Second Defense of the English People, The Reason of Church Government, Of Education,* and *The Doctrine and Discipline of Divorce*. On one level, this chapter participates in an ongoing discussion of the structure of *Paradise Lost*, but here structure is understood in architectural terms, rather than narrative terms as is usually the case.[4] For example, when Burton Jasper Weber "present[s] a scheme for explaining the structure of the poem," he defines *structure* as "how its two plots are related, what place the minor characters have." Similarly, Ralph Waterbury Condee explains, "By structure I mean that quality of a literary work which gives it its most special character of thrust, movement, or progression."[5] This chapter's consideration of what is usually referred to as the structure of *Paradise Lost* takes seriously Milton's own reflections on architecture (and refers instead to the poem's form). These references are then used to read the various architectures of *Paradise Lost*: Pandæmonium, the Blissful Bower, and the poem itself.

Ironically, architectural references to *Paradise Lost* may even be older than the poem; in *The Second Defense of the English People*, Milton refers to the work of "the epic poet," declaring "I have delivered my testimony, I would almost say, have erected a monument."[6] Milton here figures himself as an architect. Rather than the two built spaces within the poem— what Marcia Pointon calls "the landscape of Eden and the architecture of Hell"—I am more interested in the poem's overall structure, particularly the difference between its form in 1667 and that in 1674, when Milton increased the number of books from ten to twelve, a change that has occasioned much speculation, in part as it seems to constitute "Milton's last recorded comment on his poem."[7] Considered in seventeenth-century architectural terms, *Paradise Lost* represents what Milton calls "a kind of eccentrical equation," one which, while admitting the poem's fallen nature, may still indicate its relationship with a universal, unfallen structure.[8] If the 1667 edition "hangs off in an unclosing proportion," the revised 1674 version may instead have been "framed with more Equity," to borrow a description from the *Doctrine and Discipline of Divorce*.[9]

Although this chapter focuses on its possibly proportionate structure, like William Kerrigan "I am unable to read *Paradise Lost* as a comfortably orthodox poem" and instead see its proportionate structure as a rhetorical strategy that Milton employs in the context of the Restoration, and as more a literary strategy than a theological one at that. In this reading, then, what Lana Cable calls "Milton's classicism" should not be construed as an unmediated "affirmation of seemingly eternal human values," although it may be a clever and important appeal to them. On the one hand, Milton's interest in structure is consistent with that curious mix of "radical" politics and "fundamentally motivating belief in reason" that Joan Bennett describes. On the other, of course, it is in part because of these structural elements that "Milton's *Paradise Lost* is no pamphlet," as Sharon Achinstein reminds us.[10]

Rather than a commitment to an unchanging, orthodox position,

Milton's use of architectural images in the pamphlets (perhaps drawing on the conventional association between the spiritual Church and the physical structure of churches) indicates changes in his attitude toward events between 1642 and 1660. In 1642's *The Reason of Church Government*, Milton argues that "God, whenever he meant to reform his church, never intended to leave the government thereof, delineated in such curious architecture, to be patched afterwards."[11] The spiritual Church, like any actual church, should be well conceived, and well built: watertight, in a word. But by 1654, during the Commonwealth, Milton had become concerned that future generations might "see that the foundations were well laid . . . but with deep emotions of concern will they regret that those were wanting who might have completed the structure," as he writes in *The Second Defense of the English People*.[12] By 1660, the year of the Restoration, Milton's architectural references acquire an added urgency: "What will they say of us and of the whole English name but scoffingly, as of that foolish builder, mentioned by our Saviour, who began to build a tower and was not able to finish it?"[13] These three quotes indicate that Milton's architectural references, far from being uncomplicated classical references to unchanging Christian values, are increasingly oppositional, having to do with what he calls "the reforming of reformation itself."[14]

Milton's familiarity with classical architectural theory can be seen in *Of Education* (1644, 1673), where he recommends that students read Vitruvius's *De architectura*, probably the single most important architectural text of the Renaissance. Alberti responds to it, Palladio illustrates it, and in England, Wotton summarizes it; across Europe and over several centuries, Vitruvius and the Vitruvian treatment of architecture recur. By placing Vitruvius's *De architectura* "after . . . the principles of arithmetic . . . astronomy, and geography," Milton follows the Vitruvian arrangement, seeing architecture as participating through mathematics in the universal (here represented by astronomy and geography).[15] This connection between architecture, mathematics, and the cosmos, strange as it may

seem to those today familiar with the Modernist combination of architecture and engineering, was typical in the seventeenth century.

In *De architectura* Vitruvius grounds his universalist architectural
theory by positing an original, natural, primitive architecture, upon
which all subsequent architecture is based:

> Once upon a time . . . trees . . . tossed by storms and winds and rubbing
> their branches together, kindled a fire. Terrified . . . those who were about
> that place . . . put to flight. Afterwards when the thing was quieted down,
> approaching nearer, they perceived that the advantage was great. . . .
> Therefore, because of the discovery of fire . . . Many came together into
> one place. . . . After thus meeting together, they began . . . to make shel-
> ters of leaves imitating the nests of swallows and their methods of build-
> ing. . . . With upright forked props and twigs put between, they wove
> their walls. (2.1.1–4)

Not only did people come together and build only after an initial cata-
strophic fire, their original architecture was woven, in imitations of birds'
nests.

This original architecture naturalizes Vitruvius's essentially
Pythagorean theory, creating an anthropological or historical base for
architecture's ability to imitate nature. The same is true for what is perhaps the most famous passage from *De architectura* (much more famous
for how it has been drawn than for how it reads)—a circle inscribed
around an outstretched body (known as "the Vitruvian man"): "For if a
man lies on his back with his hands and feet outspread, and the center of
a circle is placed in his navel, his figure and toes will be touched by the
circumference. . . . to the outstretched hands, the breadth will be found
equal to the height" (3.1.3). This image neatly represents Vitruvius's claim
that mathematical ratios are natural: "Nature has so planned the human
body that the face from the Chin to the top of the forehead . . . is a tenth

part," and "the other limbs also have their own proportionate measurements" (3.1.2). But the point is not simply that "man is the measure of all things." Rather, the Vitruvian man's measurement participates in the ratios that measure all things.

Proportion, which Vitruvius calls *analogia*, has to do with the similarities or the likenesses of parts across a structure and is described in terms of the human body: a building should "have an exact proportion worked out after the fashion of the members of a finely-shaped human body" (3.1.1). For Vitruvius, this claim is consistent with the "Pythagoreans'" (2.2.1) argument that numbers represent the inner workings of the natural world, that "numbers were not only quantities; they were qualities as well."[16] Following this Pythagorean line, Vitruvius argues that "buildings should have their designs determined by the proportions of a fixed unit," whereby the fixed unit, or module, provides a basis of measurement against which the proportions, or ratios, between the various parts of a building can be established.[17] The proportions thus established by the fixed unit allow the building to participate in the same universal, natural order represented by the birds in the story of the original architecture. It is probably important for the revised edition of *Paradise Lost* that Vitruvius applies this type of proportionate architecture particularly to religious building: "The planning of temples depends upon symmetry" (3.1.1).

Milton's *Reason of Church Government* alludes to this Vitruvian analogy, describing "the soul of man" as "his rational temple" and wondering whether "the divine square and compass thereof form and regenerate us." The bodily proportion analogy, and of course the circle and the square, replay the image of the Vitruvian man. Moreover, Milton goes on to add an important term, arguing that this shaping is designed "to edify . . . Christ's body, which is his church, in all her glorious lineaments."[18] We already have seen Milton argue that "the Church" should be proportionate, but the notion that a church has "lineaments" entails the usage of a word developed by Leon Battista Alberti, whose *Art of Building* (1450) begins with a discussion of architectural *lineamenta*, which Alberti uses self-consciously to distinguish his treatise from that of Vitruvius. "Lineaments" could refer solely to clothing, but, like Alberti, Milton uses it in connection with temple, square, and compass, all of which suggest the architectural implication, whether or not Milton had read Alberti.

Although Alberti, like Vitruvius, argues that "beauty is that reasoned harmony of all the parts within a body"—i.e., that structures are beautiful if they replicate the form of an idealized, proportionate body—Alberti also differs significantly from Vitruvius. By drawing on a tradition of medieval and Renaissance numerology unavailable to Vitruvius, Alberti seizes upon the implied musical implications of "reasoned harmony" and expands upon Vitruvius's understanding of proportionate, mathematical, and natural ratios:

> That Nature is composed of threes all philosophers agree. And as for the number five, when I consider the many varied and wonderful things that either themselves relate to that number or are produced by something that contains it—such as the human hand—I do not think it wrong that it should be called divine, and rightly to be dedicated to the gods of the arts, and Mercury in particular. And as for the number seven, it is clear that the great maker of all things, God, is particularly delighted by it, in that he has made seven planets to wander the heavens, and has so regulated man, his favorite creature, that conception, formation, adolescence, maturity, and so on, all these stages he has made reducible to seven. . . . Another popular odd number was nine, that of the orbs which provident Nature has set in the sky. . . . The sixfold is one of the very few which is called "perfect," because it is the sum of all integral divisors [1, 2, 3]. . . . Aristotle thought the tenth the most perfect number of all; perhaps, as some interpret, because its square equals the cube of four consecutive numbers.[19]

Alberti's point is still Vitruvian: proportions shape the beautiful by allowing it to participate in the universal, numerical order, but now the range of possibly significant numbers includes almost every integer between 1 and 10.[20] For Alberti, this newly numerological understanding means that "it is absolutely certain that Nature is wholly consistent," meaning that numbers are both the cause and the evidence of nature's consistency. Those numbers can be heard in music and seen in architecture: "The very same numbers that cause sounds . . . can also fill the eyes and mind with wondrous delight."[21] Alberti's explanation then is not merely analogical; it is not that music and architecture are alike. They are the same in that they are both grounded in, and understood as part of, a universal numerical order.

Like Vitruvius's *De architectura*, Alberti's treatise also includes a story about an original architecture, although Alberti's differs from Vitruvius's as much as their numerical theories do. In keeping with the differentiation between the various perfect numbers and their varied reasons for perfection, Alberti's original architecture is also highly specialized, emphasizing privacy for the inhabitants and social and programmatic distinctions. "Not wishing to have all their household and private affairs conducted in the same place, they set aside one space for sleeping, another for the hearth, and allocated other spaces for other uses."[22] Although it would seem to be a structural point, Alberti's argument—that "they built walls on which a roof could be laid," and that they only subsequently "opened windows and doors in the walls"—emphasizes exclusion and separation.

Alberti also begins with a biblical reference, "In the beginning,"[23] which would have been unknown to Vitruvius, and which makes possible further expansions of classical architectural theory. In 1624 Sir Henry Wotton published *The Elements of Architecture*, the only English-language architectural treatise of the first half of the seventeenth century, and a book whose "reputation . . . as a classic statement of architectural funda-

mentals lasted far into the eighteenth century."[24] In it he refers to both
Alberti and Vitruvius: "Our principal Master is Vitruvius"; Alberti is
"from the Schoole of Pythagoras (where it was fundamentall *Maxime*,
that the Images of all things are latent in *Numbers*)." And there are many
ways in which Wotton follows them quite specifically in arguing for the
connections between "arte," "Harmony," "Proportions," and "Nature." For
example, like Alberti, Wotton brings together the auditory and the
visual, the musical and the architectural—"reducing *Symmetrie* to *Symphonie*, and the *harmonie* of Sounde, to a kinde of *harmonie* in *Sight*."[25]

But in the same way that Alberti emended Vitruvius, expanding the
list of philosophically significant numbers, Wotton, rather than simply
reiterating Vitruvius's and Alberti's Pythagorean assumptions about
rational systems, also contributes to their work. For example, rather than
isolating any number itself, Wotton claims that there are instead two significant harmonic proportions: "The two principall Consonances, that
most ravish the Eare, are by consent of all Nature, the proportion
between two and three. The other from the double Intervalle, betweene
One and Two, or betweene Two and foure, &c." The latter of these two
is represented by 1:2, or 2:4, a point which becomes very important with
the 1674 edition of *Paradise Lost*. Wotton also adds the language of seventeenth-century science, arguing that an architect, by virtue of this system of harmonic proportions, is "a *Diver* into *Causes* and into the *Myster-
ies of Proportion*." Most importantly, Wotton's formulation builds on
Alberti's biblical reference. It is not simply that numbers symbolically
represent the universal order; they give access to what controls the events
in that system: "The *High Architect* of the world, had displaid . . . skill."[26]
For Wotton, "God" identifies whoever designed this universe, whose
image—both "God"'s and the universe's—can be seen in the proportioned and harmonic and is described as architecture.

Consequently, Wotton argues that "Truth . . . is a Just and Naturall
Proportion," an understanding of truth which relies on the Vitruvian

notion of natural proportion and also invokes a relatively new term: *just*.[27] This word, which might usually be taken to refer to justice, is no less an architectural term; it could apply, for example, to masonry or stonework or to how walls and joints fit together. Perhaps because of its original association with "jousting" and "things coming together," *just* implies, as the *Oxford English Dictionary* explains, "so as to fit exactly; in a close-fitting way." Labeling this meaning now archaic, the *OED* gives only sixteenth- and seventeenth-century examples of this architectural-masonry use (including one from Etheredge), indicating that it was still part of the word's usage at the time of the publication of *Paradise Lost*. Moreover, even if Wotton's "Just" refers to justice, he considers justice in architectural terms (either "Proportion" or "Just"), making the distinction between the two meanings even more difficult to establish. "Justifying," of course, figures prominently in Milton's *Paradise Lost*. Milton's "justification"—both his use of the term and his attempt to "justify"—conveys an architectural resonance.

In 1638, as he arranged his upcoming visit to Italy, Milton contacted Sir Henry Wotton. By the time they met, fourteen years had passed since Wotton's book was published, more than enough time for Milton to have heard of and read the book and for his esteem of Wotton to have increased. In *The Second Defense* Milton recalls that Wotton "gave me a signal proof of his regard . . . breathing not only the warmest friendship, but containing some maxims of conduct which I found very useful in my travels." With Wotton's advice for his itinerary, Milton left England and traveled to the Continent in 1638, spending most of his time in Italy, including visits to Genoa, Pisa, Florence, Siena, Rome, Naples, and Venice. Milton pointed out that the trip to Italy allowed him a sustained opportunity to learn about Italian, or more specifically, Roman, architecture. He went to Rome and "spent about two months in viewing the antiquities of that renowned city."[28] Prominent among the antiquities were the buildings of ancient Rome, that is, *antiquities* defined in the *OED* as "remains or monuments of antiquity."

Christopher Hill believes that "the fifteen months of Milton's Italian journey are of crucial importance in his intellectual development."[29] In the context of what James Ackerman calls "Renaissance architectural practice," Milton's "viewing the antiquities" has something other than a touristic, amateuristic connotation. In the Renaissance, viewing the antiquities was an integral part of architectural education, as can be seen, for example, in the careers of Palladio or Inigo Jones. According to Ackerman, "The essential prerequisite for the practice of architecture was a knowledge of Roman remains. This was gained at first hand whenever possible, not only in Rome itself, but throughout Italy and Provence."[30] In other words, Milton's trip gave him, among other things, the best training then available for a young architect, while his two months in Rome indicate the extent and quality of his architectural education.

In 1642, only a few years after returning from Italy (and twenty-five years before first publishing *Paradise Lost*), when Milton referred to his Italian trip, he associated it with his interest in writing an epic: "In the private academies of Italy, whither I was favored to resort . . . an inward prompting . . . grew daily upon me . . . that what the greatest and choicest wits of Athens, Rome, or modern Italy, and those Hebrews of old did for their country, I . . . might do for mine." The trip to Italy represents a kind of inspiration for what would become *Paradise Lost*, and it is important that Milton should go on to say, regarding his interest in writing an epic, that "I, in my proportion . . . might [write such a work]"; not only does his interest in an English epic emerge during his trip to Italy, but to describe it he subsequently uses a term—*proportion*—central to Renaissance architectural theory.[31] In other words, Milton's declaration regarding his future epic joins Renaissance architectural practice (his visit to Italy and his viewing the antiquities) and theory ("proportion").

In its conflation of the natural and the supernatural, Milton's use of "discipline" in *The Reason of Church Government* is also similar to what we have seen in Renaissance architectural theory. The important point is not merely that Milton used architectural images or metaphors to shape

his arguments, but that these architectural references bring together literary structure, architecture, and Milton's idea of a church. This combination can be seen in Milton's description of Paul's epistles (and the
point could also apply to the claim made by the form of *Paradise Lost*): "a
heavenly structure of evangelic discipline, so diffusive of knowledge . . .
that it cannot be wondered if that elegant and artful symmetry of the
promised new temple in Ezekiel . . . were made to signify the inward
beauty and splendor of the Christian church thus governed."[32] This passage relies on architectural terms such as *structure* and *temple* and invokes
terms associated with classical and Renaissance architectural theory,
such as *symmetry*, to suggest that the physical church "signifies" the invisible beauty of the inward state of the church believers. If "thus governed"
suggests how the Church might be envisioned in the epistles of Paul,
such governance, within the passage, is possible only with "discipline";
neither "government" nor "discipline" as Milton uses them, however,
should be understood apart from the more explicitly architectural "symmetry" that Milton claims characterizes Paul's epistles. Unlike recent discussions of discipline, which understand it in terms of punishing the
human body into an unnatural conformity, Milton, perhaps expanding
the representation implicit in something like the Vitruvian man, compares discipline to "a golden surveying reed" which, as a "line and level,"
"marks out and measures"—references not to the "surveillance" of the
human subject but rather to a "surveyor" (who helps to site a building).[33]

Moreover, discipline is, according to Milton, "not only the removal of
disorder" but, "if any visible shape can be given to divine things, the very
visible shape and image of virtue."[34] Like architectural proportion as
understood in Renaissance architectural theory, discipline makes the
invisible visible; as do the mathematical ratios implied across the façade
of a building, discipline can indicate a relationship with a universal order.
In a recent study S. K. Heninger Jr. makes a point regarding ratio that
also applies to Milton's idea of discipline: "*Ratio* makes knowable the oth

erwise inaccessible subtext of form."[35] Like architectural ratios, discipline is, for Milton, "seen in the regular . . . motions of . . . heavenly paces."[36] Discipline, like a well-designed building, combines "shape," "regular[ity]," and "harmony." In its relationship to order, geometry, carpentry, and the divine, it is discipline that helps a human structure participate in the universal.

As it was with discipline, making the invisible visible is precisely the predicament that is faced in *Paradise Lost*—by the narrator, by Raphael, and perhaps by Milton as well. Like the narrator, Renaissance architectural theory argues that the structure of a well-designed building can "see and tell / Of things invisible to mortal sight," principally the supposedly universal patterns of reason.[37] For *Paradise Lost*, the problem is how to represent something—the war in Heaven, Eden, the Fall, etc.—that no human can really know. Raphael refers to this problem as "what surmounts the reach / Of human sense" and says he "shall delineate so, / By lik'ning spiritual to corporeal forms" (5.571–73). In other words, it is by a process of analogy, by "lik'ning," that Raphael intends to indicate what might reside beyond the "reach of human sense." He proceeds by what Vitruvius calls *analogia*. Essentially, analogy—or, in Pythagorean terms, proportion—allows, by setting up a comparison, an approximate representation of the otherwise unrepresentable.

This sense of analogy, of comparison, applies to both of the epic's two principal spaces, Pandæmonium and the Blissful Bower, and to *Paradise Lost* itself. The two built environments represent a series of dichotomies developed through Renaissance architectural theory: original vs. classical; natural vs. rule-bound; divine vs. human. The two spaces also represent, in Milton's terms, the difference between the unfallen and the fallen or between God and Satan. According to architectural theory *Paradise Lost* itself should somehow recoup the difference between the human and the divine, between the visible and the invisible, between the spiritual and the corporal, and between the classical and the natural; in order to do so, it too operates with a principle of *analogia*, a principle of proportion.

Architecturally, the poem invites a comparison between its two built spaces: Pandæmonium and the Bower of Bliss. Consider, for example, the description of building Pandæmonium in book 1:

> Anon out of the earth a fabric huge
> Rose like an Exhaltation, with the sound
> Of Dulcet symphonies and voices sweet,
> Built like a Temple, where *Pilasters* round
> Were set, and Doric pillars overlaid
> With Golden Architrave; nor did there want
> Cornice or Frieze, with bossy Sculptures grav'n;
> The Roof was fretted Gold. (1.710–17)

Words such as "Pilaster," "Doric," "Architrave," "Cornice," and "Frieze" suggest the narrator's familiarity with what Summerson calls "the language of classical architecture."[38] Because it would seem that the fallen angels are remarkably able to build very quickly the kind of buildings Europeans admire, the question then becomes how to read this building. Is it, to put it bluntly, good or bad? In many ways this evaluative question is precisely what the poem forces readers to ask, about everything. It is nonetheless interesting that that question should emerge so early and with reference to a specifically architectural production.

When considering either what valence this "Temple" might have in the poem, or relatedly, how one might be able to determine that valence, it is significant that "Mammon led them on" to build the temple (1.678). As the narrator describes him, Mammon is "the least erected Spirit that fell" (1.679), a description that suggests a whole series of impotencies, including of course the architectural connotation of falling buildings.

Moreover, the angels' choice of the Doric order may itself give the reader an index of value. The Doric order is gendered: male, according to the tradition initially recorded by Vitruvius. This gendered association becomes particularly important when one considers the violence with which the angels acquire materials for their temple. Mammon taught them to "ransack . . . the center, and . . . Rifl[e] . . . the bowels of thir mother Earth" (1.684–87). Ripping, penetrating, and rifling a "mother"—rape. By the time the fallen angels "Op'n'd into the Hill a spacious wound / And digg'd out ribs of Gold" (1.688–90), the violence of the image is accentuated by what has preceded it.

The use of the word *rib* alludes to Adam's recollection of Eve's birth: a "shape . . . op'n'd my left side, and took from thence a rib" (8.462–69), and this repetition of "rib" invites a reconsideration of Pandæmonium. The creation of Eve dramatizes what we might call a truly natural archi-tecture, with the person whom Wotton and *Paradise Lost* refer to as the "High" or "Great" architect creating not another building but another being. By the eighth book words like "rib" and "exhalation," which are used to describe the building of both Pandæmonium and Eve, have acquired another, less fallen resonance.

If Eve represents a kind of building, there is a Miltonic irony implicit in "Sin" saying to "Satan," "O . . . prime Architect. . . . Thy Virtue hath won / What thy hands builded not" (10.352–64). Unlike God's creations, Satan's buildings are not actually built by Satan. Moreover, they are built according to the classical prescription; the narrator's description of Pandæmonium relies on the terms of classical architecture, an architec-ture self-consciously attempting to find a way of mimicking a preexis-tent, natural architecture. By using its vocabulary, the narrator is remind-ing the reader of formal, rule-bound quality of that architecture.

By contrast, the narrator describes Adam and Eve's "blissful bower" (4.691) as a place

Chos'n by the sovran Planter,

when he fram'd

All things to man's delightful use;

the roof

. . . was inwoven shade

. . . Of firm and fragrant leaf;

. . . bushy shrub

Fenc'd up the verdant wall;

each beauteous flow'r

. . . wrought

Mosaic. (4.691–701)

Of course, the description draws on and is informed by a Renaissance tradition of the *locus amoenus*, including most immediately Spenser's contribution. Nonetheless, I would argue that, perhaps especially in the architectural context, Milton uses this space as part of his own particular argument. Redolent as much with architectural theory as it is with flowers, this description of the Blissful Bower constitutes a natural architecture and in so doing invokes the extended discussion of an original architecture. Milton's description of the Blissful Bower echoes Vitruvius's original architecture: where Vitruvius argues that humans "wove" their original walls, Milton's narrator describes the roof of the Blissful Bower, which shelters the "prime of men" (5.563), as being "inwoven" (694). But Milton's rendition of this architectural trope radically literalizes the notion of a natural, original architecture. It is almost as if Milton were responding to the Vitruvian discussion of architectural origins by representing an architecture so natural that it is available only to the "prime" humans and is constituted by shrubs that grow themselves into a wall.

The description of the Blissful Bower also mentions how it was "fram'd," a term referring to other architectural figures with which Milton has peppered the poem and setting up a whole series of not necessarily architectural connections. For example, in his attempt to describe reason to Eve, Adam says that it "frames" the "Aery shapes" that "Fancy" "forms" (5.106, 105, 102, and 105). Adam's explanation of reasoning turns on the meaning of the word *frame*, and other uses of the same word in *Paradise Lost* suggest that it should be understood architecturally. In addition to the narrator contending, for example, that the Edenic Blissful Bower was "fram'd" by "the sovran Planter" (4.691–92), Adam describes the world as "this goodly Frame" (8.15), and Raphael calls God "the great Architect" (8.72).

According to Adam, it is reason that frames the results of the "Fancy," a term which, according to Wotton, "is wild and irregular."[39] In Eden, reason makes things regular for human understanding. And it does so by framing them, by giving them a shape. Or as Adam says, it does so by "joining or disjoining" them (5.106). As we have already seen, "just"-ness has to do with how things come together, or as Adam might say, how things are joined. Dayton Haskin, in his recent book on *Milton's Burden of Interpretation*, points out that the humanist logic of "framing" included "the selection, rearrangement, and assimilation of texts."[40] It is important that the activity of judging information, to which Haskin refers, is described by a metaphor such as "framing." If "framing" is understood as either shaping or building, why should it be an appropriate metaphor for the activity of reasoning? In Eden reason and justice are related by the frame. Reason and justice are related by the natural architecture.

In their conjunction of reason, architecture, and the "Frame," these passages invite an architectural understanding, not only of the humanist activity of arranging texts but of *Paradise Lost* itself. If, briefly, "the great Architect" created a "goodly Frame" within which reason can operate, or frame the forms of fancy, then by association the capacity of human reason to frame participates in the supernatural, or in the universal frame. This humanist language of framing—a language of architecture, or of how a mind's activity can reflect an overarching structure—thus requires that *Paradise Lost*, if it is to appear reasonable, be "fram'd" in such a way as to indicate its relationship with the universal architecture.

The architectural terms associated with Eden—*frame, reason, fancy, nature,* and *prime*, among others—set up parameters for "unfallen" understanding. If the Blissful Bower represents the ideal, natural, unfallen building that an architecture must imitate, then words like *frame* suggest a mechanism, albeit a prelapsarian one, for achieving that imitation. The solution to the fall would seem to have something to do with framing, with how things are arranged or ordered. If reason frames, just like God—"the Great Architect"—did in building the Blissful Bower, then humans, in reasoning, may even become God-like precisely by framing, by doing some of the Great Architect's work. In this process of evaluating Pandæmonium and the Blissful Bower, the poem has essentially invited the reader to make comparisons: between Mammon and the other angels; between the Doric and the other architectural orders; between two uses of "ribs" and, consequently, between the two prime architects.

Although we have so far focused on Raphael's storytelling, Raphael is not the only storyteller within the poem. There is also the voice of the invocations, a voice which appears in the twelve-book edition at the beginnings of books 1, 3, 7, and 9. Walter Schindler contends that "perhaps in no other epic are the invocations so structurally significant."[41] In these passages, this voice, like Raphael (and Milton), is self-consciously involved in storytelling. And unlike Raphael, or like Milton, this narrator admits its fallen state, its humanness. If Raphael represents the "divine" narrator within the poem, the invocation's voice represents the specifically "human" narrator of the poem.

As we have seen, proportion works by analogy, and for neo-

Pythagoreans it indicates an object's participation in the universal, rational, mathematical order. According to George Hersey, for the Pythagoreans "the perfect number, like a cubic number, is the goal of a progression that achieves a stable value lying outside the progression itself."[42] Structurally, in *Paradise Lost* Milton uses the proportion of the narrator's invocations to indicate his (fallen) poem's truthful relation to that (unfallen) universal order. The poem's structural proportion indicates a relation between the poem and "a stable value lying outside" the poem itself. In this sense, that the form could represent something stable outside of itself, Stanley Fish rightly points out that the poem's "outer or physical form, [is] . . . obtrusive, incidental and even irrelevant."[43] For Fish, form is to be understood merely as a vehicle for the reader's self-apprehension; once that understanding has occurred, the form is no longer important. But as we have seen with reference to architectural theory, this point would apply to most Renaissance theories of form; form matters only insofar as it leads to something else. And if the reader learns through it, then form is important, precisely for that reason.

Milton published the ten-book version of *Paradise Lost* in 1667 and seven years later published a revised, only slightly expanded twelve-book edition of the poem. In his recent work on the poem's changes, R. G. Moyles explains that with the twelve-book edition, "Book 7 has been divided into Book 7 and 8 . . . Book 8 has become 9; 9 has become 10; and Book 10 has been divided into 11 and 12." The question is what might be preferable about the new twelve-book arrangement, or to put it another way, what the changes did to the poem, particularly considering that the revision added only nine lines to the original ten-book poem.[44]

In terms of content, therefore, the poem seems to have changed very little. But in changing the poem's books, Milton had changed the poem's proportion and its structure. For the twelve-book structure changes the placement of the invocations and thus, by changing the place of the narrator, changes the place of the human; it changes the place of the fallen.

In the ten-book version the invocations occur at the beginnings of books 1, 3, 7, and 8. With this ten-book structure, the invocations occur at intervals of 2, 4, 1—i.e., disproportionately. Therefore, the ten-book edition of the poem does not establish an even proportion between the invocations—it "hangs off in an unclosing proportion."[45]

In the twelve-book edition, by breaking up book 8 and converting book 8 into book 9, Milton moves an invocation to the beginning of book 9, so that in the twelve-book edition, the invocations occur at the beginnings of books 1, 3, 7, and 9. As a consequence, in this version the invocations occur at intervals of 2, 4, 2. This ratio, of 1:2, is one of Wotton's preferred proportions. It is also known as a diapason and is referred to as such in Milton's "At a Solemn Music," a poem about how "disproportion'd sin" ended that "melodious noise" that nature once sang. That unfallen sound is described as a "perfect Diapason," a ratio of 1 to 2. If we add the amount of *Paradise Lost* remaining from the beginning of book 9 to the end of book 12, we get intervals approximating 2, 4, 2, 4. Consequently, with the revision up to twelve books, the poem no longer hangs off in an unclosing disproportion (fig. 1).

In a way, we are looking at the plan, in the architectural sense of the word, of *Paradise Lost*, which was written at a time when "the plan dominated architecture as never before or since."[46] Renaissance architectural theory reads the plan as a series of spatial units; it was "an age when all art was thought of spatially."[47] These modules are frequently marked as such in architectural drawings, providing contemporary support for this kind of reading.[48] In a classic example, Francesco di Giorgio, a fifteenth-century Italian architect, illustrates his *Trattato* showing a human figure overlaid with a cruciform plan, on which a series of parallel spaces are indicated by alphabetical markings.[49] Similarly, Tzonis and Lefaivre in a recent work show how one might "segment [a] plan into the following seven parts: A B C D C B A," which, by an associative principle, they further reduce to "A B A."[50]

Paradise Lost acknowledges several times the possibility of this proportionate, mathematical reading. At the beginning of book 7, the narrator reminds us of proportionate ratios and intervals, saying that "half yet remains unsung" (7.21). In book 3 the narrator hopes to present "harmonious numbers" (37). In book 5 the proof of Adam and Eve's unfallen linguistic ability is their "prompt eloquence" and its consequent ability easily to produce "numerous Verse" (150). With phrases such as "harmonious numbers" and "numerous verse," the narrator is hearkening back to the Renaissance belief in a connection between numbers, harmony, and poetry, or what Wotton calls "reducing Symmetrie to Symphonie."

That Milton was self-conscious about the metrical structure has already been argued by critics such as Lee M. Johnson who have studied, among other things, the structure of the poem's first invocation. Because, as Johnson points out, "it divides asymmetrically into two parts: (1) a sixteen-line sentence . . . followed by (2) a ten-line sentence," this invocation "expresses the symbolic value of what is known as the 'divine proportion,'"

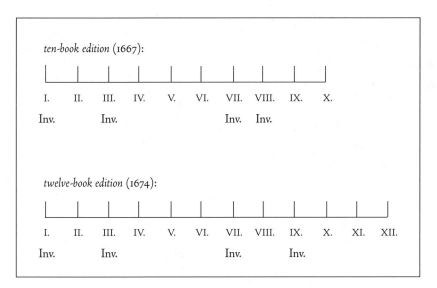

1. Comparison of invocations in the 1667 and 1674 editions of *Paradise Lost*

a relationship between two parts in which the smaller (*a*) is to the larger (*b*) as the larger is to the whole (*a* + *b*): A:B::B:(A + B); or in the case of the invocation, 10:16::16:26. In other words, Johnson shows that the proportion of the first invocation participates in the universal, rational order. Or as Johnson contends, the invocation "suggests a close correlation between the mathematical symbolism of his style and the theological nature of his subject." According to Johnson, the golden section of the first invocation—the proportion—represents "an ideal form [by means of which] an actual structure, . . . although always falling short of the ideal, takes whatever meaning it has from its conjunction with that form."

Johnson argues that "by emphasizing the formal construction of Milton's invocations in *Paradise Lost*, we can perceive how essential his non-verbal artistry is to his verbal meaning."[51] I agree, but I would argue that the invocations must be considered in their relationship to the poem as a whole, especially in the wake of the revision from a ten-book to a twelve-book form. Milton frames the structure of *Paradise Lost* to achieve an imitation of that unfallen, numerical verse. Structurally, Milton attempts to tap into what Wittkower describes as a "harmonic perfection of the geometrical scheme [which] represents an absolute value, independent of our subjective and transitory perception."[52] In Renaissance architectural theory, proportion is what would allow him to do that. In the words of Wotton, "Truth . . . is a Just and Naturall Proportion." The twelve-book edition of *Paradise Lost* changes the ratios with which the human, or the representative of the human, intervenes in the poem as a whole.

Wotton concludes his architectural treatise by claiming that he is working on another book, *A Philosophical Survey of Education*, "which," he argues, "is indeed, a second *building*, or repairing of Nature . . . a kinde of *Morall Architecture*."[53] Of course, the idea that education might repair nature by giving us a moral architecture is important to Milton, according to whom "the end of learning is to repair the ruins of our first parents."[54] Wotton's idea of a therapeutic "Morall Architecture" produced by education is akin to Milton's idea of the soul's rational temple being surveyed by the divine compass of discipline. If, as Wotton defines it, truth is a just and natural proportion, then *Paradise Lost* is a kind of moral architecture.

While narrating for Adam God's creation (framing?) of the universe, Raphael contends that God designed in such a way as to avoid "the loud misrule," because God knew that "fierce extremes / contiguous might distemper the whole frame" (271–73). Raphael thus, in one sentence, suggests that the universe is architectural ("frame"), and that its spatialization is an important moral issue. That is, Raphael argues that if fierce extremes are placed "contiguous," or near each other, a distempering will occur. Or to put it more positively, a proper, tempered spatialization, by the Great Architect, helps avoid the "the loud misrule of Chaos." A just framing, a judicious use of reason, becomes a spatial issue. It may be that just such a concern for the judicious use of space motivates the 1674 rearrangement of *Paradise Lost*, for this eccentrical equation allows Milton to place the actual structure of *Paradise Lost* somewhere between Pandæmonium and the Blissful Bower. That is, the form of this particular epic poem—the last epic, all about the very beginning—likens, as Raphael would say, spiritual to corporal forms.

"Against the Too Exact Observance of the Rules": Vanbrugh's Drama and Architecture

2

β THE CAREERS OF SIR JOHN VANBRUGH, author of *The Relapse* and *The Provok'd Wife* and architect at Castle Howard and Blenheim Palace, provide an inviting opportunity to consider the relationships between literature and architecture. Between 1696 and 1705 playwriting and producing occupied Vanbrugh's professional life, while in 1699 Castle Howard was his first major architectural commission. By 1703 Vanbrugh had become the Comptroller of the Works, "the second highest architectural post in England"; he worked as an architect for the rest of his life.[1] Because his theatrical and architectural practices seem to have been more or less sequential—as Swift quipped, "Van's genius, without thought or lecture / Is hugely turned to architecture"—Sir John Vanbrugh also presents a unique challenge.[2] On the one hand, "we have tended," as Laurence Whistler writes, "to regard him as a brilliantly successful dramatist who suddenly turned to architecture," and on the other, it is tempting to employ Vanbrugh's architecture, presumably his mature work, to describe his plays, as if one represented the fuller, more complete version of the other.[3] But it is also possible that Vanbrugh's literature offers a way of understanding his architecture, and that, consequently, they can be seen together, as related, similar activities that simply happen to have occupied Vanbrugh at different times in his life.

This chapter considers two of Vanbrugh's productions, one literary (*The Provok'd Wife*) and one architectural (the Queen's/Haymarket Theatre), and contemporary responses to them. Coming as they do at the beginning and the end, respectively, of his ten–year relationship with theater, these two works represent important examples of Vanbrugh's transition from literature to architecture and show how Vanbrugh's architectural interests can be seen in his literature, or conversely, how his literary interests can be seen in his architectural practice. Because both *The Provok'd Wife* and the Haymarket Theatre were soundly criticized after their completion, *The Provok'd Wife* being singled out by Jeremy Collier in his *A Short View of the Immorality and Profaneness of the English Stage*, and the Haymarket Theatre (which had to be entirely renovated only three years after its opening) discussed unsympathetically in Colley Cibber's *Apology for the Life of Colley Cibber*, there is a contemporary critical vocabulary with which it is possible to measure Vanbrugh's style.[4] Moreover, the similarities between Collier's criticism of the play and Cibber's criticism of the theater remind us once again how closely related were literary and architectural understanding in the late seventeenth century.

Flexibly reading architectural terms associated with *The Provok'd Wife* and Collier's criticism of it recovers the political contest over aesthetic form that followed Vanbrugh through his various projects, literary or architectural. For this first critical controversy makes explicit much that is important in Vanbrugh's careers as author and as architect: arguments over the rules, over natural orderliness, over proportion, and over whether there are any naturally proportionate political arrangements. The repetition of similar themes in these critiques of Vanbrugh's work, despite the seeming difference of the media, supports seeing a relationship between his literature and his architecture. What is known as the Collier Controversy should be understood as but the first specific instance of a conflict that repeats itself several times in Vanbrugh's careers; Collier's critique of the plays, for example, recurs in Cibber's critique of the theater. These contemporary terms make it possible to recover Vanbrugh without relying on conventional literary or architectural historical typologies (Vanbrugh is no more baroque, for instance, than Milton or Hawksmoor, although he differs from them in many significant ways that such an adjective does not indicate).

Considered generally, the conflict between Vanbrugh and Collier, or between Vanbrugh and Cibber, represents a version of the argument over the appropriate application of the classical rules, supposedly the way to ensure a natural representation, both in drama and, as we have seen, in architecture. In *The Provok'd Wife*, a rift opens up between reason and nature, as Vanbrugh shifts away from the understanding of nature that had characterized Milton's work. However, as most of the play's characters do not delve into the implications of this rift, and the one who does is treated poorly by the others, it is important not to overestimate the difference Vanbrugh sees between reason and nature. Although it is not a Rousseauian disjunction between the two, such a shift in the meanings of nature and reason, even if it is only toyed with, is quite significant. If adhered to in architecture and drama, it means that Vanbrugh need not feel obliged to follow the classical rules.

At what would seem to represent a turning point between his two careers, Vanbrugh wrote *A Short Vindication* (1698) in response to Collier's critique. Vanbrugh's claim in this pamphlet—"I think I need trouble myself . . . little to justify"[5]—suggests ways of tying together Vanbrugh's two careers. The fact that this supposed vindication actually refuses to justify has several important consequences, not the least of them being its effective distancing of Vanbrugh's historical and formal position from Milton's. Milton claims that *Paradise Lost* will "justify the ways of God to men," and this justification entails the form of Milton's epic itself, with the poem's structure suggesting the proportionate nature of his argument's truth. Vanbrugh, on the other hand, need not trouble himself to justify. The architectural implication of the word *justify* makes it all the more interesting that Vanbrugh, who was himself becoming an architect when he wrote his *Vindication*, should not feel compelled to do so. Within the classical terms, if dramatists or architects should feel "little need to justify," their work would be characterized by "irregularities," which Collier says of Vanbrugh's plays, and Colley Cibber eventually says of his theater.

Vanbrugh had little need to justify because he was arguing for a new and different understanding of the rules, or as he writes in the *Vindication*, "I could say a great deal against the too exact observance of the Rules."[6] By the time Vanbrugh wrote this *Vindication*, *The Provok'd Wife* itself already had said a great deal against a too exact observance of the rules. But both *The Provok'd Wife* and the Haymarket Theatre indicate that ultimately Vanbrugh's opposition to such observance was a consequence of a certain understanding of the changes wrought by the 1688 Revolution. Legend, as well as some of Vanbrugh's own statements, indicates that the play might have been written much closer to 1688 than its 1698 production would indicate. In his *Vindication*, for example, Vanbrugh admits that the play was "writ many years ago, and when I was very young."[7] The play's age and his youth are two of its possible defenses; the conventions that had governed political life during the Restoration were then up for reconsideration. The circumstances surrounding its original writing and evidence within the play make *The Provok'd Wife* a dramatization of a Whiggish response to the politics of the Glorious Revolution. Although I start with the play, I also point out a similar political possibility in Vanbrugh's architecture, here represented principally by his Haymarket Theatre.

The Provok'd Wife draws on the familiar analogy of the family and the national government to retell the Whig story of how Parliament defended the British people from an absolute monarch. In this case, the unjust treatment suffered by Lady Brute at the hands of her husband, Sir

John Brute, makes the audience sympathetic to her eventual unfaithfulness toward him. Although this plot entails the "affective individualism" so often discussed regarding late seventeenth-century English drama and early eighteenth-century English novels, the specific ways in which it is represented suggest that *The Provok'd Wife* is at least as much about recent national politics as it is about any new understanding of interpersonal relationships.[8] When Sir John Brute brags, for example, in a drunken rage, "I am as absolute by my privileges as the King of France is by his prerogative," the play not only describes a bad relationship between two individuals but carefully alludes to political relationships.[9]

When Heartfree and Constant meet Sir John in St. James's Park and ask about his wife, Brute says "I believe my wife's religion will keep her honest." Heartfree asks Brute the politically loaded question, "What will make her keep her religion?" Brute answers, frankly, "Persecution: and therefore she shall have it" (2.1.241–43). Although the "it" in his answer is ambiguous—the religion of the persecutor or the persecution itself—the political implications are clear enough: the passage echoes a Whiggish perception of the Stuarts. When Lady Brute first considers the possibility of being unfaithful to her persecuting husband, she wonders: "What opposes? My matrimonial vow? Why, what did I vow? . . . to be true to my husband. . . . and he promised to be kind to me. But he hasn't kept his word. Why then I'm absolved from mine. . . . The argument's good between the king and the people, why not between the husband and the wife?" (1.1.65–72). Lady Brute here refers to and draws upon the parliamentary contractual understanding of monarchy manifested in the Revolution of 1688. Like the British people (Whiggishly understood), she has been "provok'd," and quite self-consciously like Parliament, she argues that simply because rules have the force of rule does not always mean that they need to be followed. For the Parliamentarians, rules are contractual, or conventional, and as a consequence can be and even need to be negotiated.

In conceding that "according to the strict statute law of religion I should do no wrong," Lady Brute makes explicit the degree to which following the strict statute of the law is at issue in the play. When she argues that "if there were a Court of Chancery in heaven I'm sure I should cast him," Bellinda retorts, "If there were a House of Lords you might," thus relying on the implicit governmental analogy that has characterized Lady Brute's argument so far (1.1.94–97). Bellinda is arguing, jokingly within the play, that although you might not get redress from the Court, judicial or royal, you could do so from Parliament. Discussing how Sir John treats her, Lady Fancyfull asks, "Can his faults release my duty?" to which Constant replies, "In equity, without doubt. And where laws dispense with equity, equity should dispense with laws" (4.4.165–67). In the context of a play laden with political allusions, this ethical point—if a contract means anything, it must govern both partners equally—also has a high political application, having to do with the exigencies that revolutionary situations place on participants. If the laws dispense with equity, dispense with the laws.

As Heartfree puts it, "All revolutions run into extremes," and this play seems to accept those extremes as "natural" (5.4.56). In the context of late seventeenth-century classicism, when "the Rules" were at issue in both architecture and drama, Lady Brute's possible refusal of laws has a formal corollary. That is, as a narrative in support of the parliamentary position in the Glorious Revolution of 1688, The Provok'd Wife participates in and responds to historical circumstances. Such participation, however, is not restricted to the play's narrative. If this play is concerned with extreme, revolutionary conditions, then an unmodified generic type would run counter to the argument; it would be too conventional for the circumstances. But at the same time, Vanbrugh also seems aware that if this play does vary too much from the conventions, it will strike the audience as odd. In the prologue he contends that "to write these plays, even that's to be an ass," and, equally self-consciously, "our author he's a scribbling fool" (14, 6).

Consequently, it is not only Lady Brute who must respond to Sir

John Brute within the play; the play itself must represent the supersession of the rules implied by Lady Brute's story. But that places Vanbrugh in a bind; either *The Provok'd Wife* will be too conventional for its own point, or it will be so unconventional as to make it essentially foolish. This dilemma is represented in the play by one character, Lady Fancyfull, who, as a writer and as the object of the other characters' scorn, could represent Vanbrugh's ambivalent sense of himself as an author overlooking what the rules or conventions expect. The first time the audience sees Lady Fancyfull, she is fulfilling the Prologue's definition of playwriting: the Prologue (and Vanbrugh's subsequent *Vindication*) argues that "'tis the intent and business of the stage . . . To hold to every man a faithful glass" (1–3), precisely what Lady Fancyfull is doing when she first appears in the play.

Lady Fancyfull has written a poem and appears in her apartment with a musician who has set her poetry—"A Song to be Sung between a Man and a Woman"—to music. After the musician finishes the song, Lady Fancyfull describes the origins of her poetry, or "the birth of this little dialogue": "I dreamt that by an unanimous vote I was chosen queen [of the moon]. . . . And that the first time I appeared upon my throne—all my subjects fell in love with me. Just when I waked, and seeing pen, ink, and paper lie idle upon the table, I . . . writ this impromptu" (2.2.35–42). It is difficult, of course, to take seriously this vision of a song to be sung between a man and a woman written in impromptu fashion after waking from a dream, but that is probably part of Vanbrugh's point, about himself or about unconventional writers. It is nonetheless interesting that she should be dreaming of becoming an elected monarch, rather than a hereditary one, although the fact that she is a monarch on the moon undercuts whatever self-confidence such a self-image might project.

One scene in particular enacts Vanbrugh's ambivalence. Brimming over with anger at how Heartfree treats her, Lady Fancyfull realizes that "satire has ever been of wondrous use to reform ill manners" (2.2.113). Per-

haps like Vanbrugh, Lady Fancyfull is remarkably hopeful about the efficacy of writing, but, also like Vanbrugh, her confidence does not last
long. It runs up against the problem of how people might receive the
written word. "(Sitting down to write.) Or I'll let it alone and be severe
upon him that way. (Rising up again.) Yet active severity is better than
passive. (Sitting down.) 'Tis as good let alone, for every lash I give him
perhaps he'll take for a favor. (Rising.) Yet 'tis a thousand pities so much
satire should be lost. (Sitting.) But if it should have a wrong effect upon
him 'twould distract me. (Rising.) Well I must write though after all.
(Sitting.) Or I'll let it alone, which is the same thing. (Rising)." As an
argument, what is at issue here is her sense that the "wrong effect" on the
audience would affect her. But as a play, or insofar as these lines are to be
presented on a stage, the important point lies in the stage directions. Her
repeated ups and downs literally represent her (and maybe Vanbrugh's)
nervousness about how writing will be received. At the end of this fre-
netic scene, Lady Fancyfull decides that writing and letting it alone are
"the same thing."

Like Vanbrugh's own self-conscious understanding of how a playwright is perceived (as either "ass" or "fool"), Lady Fancyfull is seen as too
headstrong and unnecessarily artificial, her authorial ambitions treated
as ludicrous. One character after another criticizes Lady Fancyfull's
appearance, dramatizing literally Vanbrugh's self-consciousness about
how people might respond to his own unusual dramatic form. However,
Lady Fancyfull represents not so much Vanbrugh's ambivalence about
writing, but rather about how a particular writing style will be received.
One character, for example, tells Lady Fancyfull that "she has vanity and
affectation enough to make her a ridiculous original in spite of all that
art and nature ever furnished" (1.1.185–87). That character contends that
such "affectation" will make her an "impertinent composition" (1.1.185).
Apparently, adding vanity and affectation to art and nature produces a
ridiculous original composition.

Another character argues that Lady Fancyfull has "undone nature by art. . . . There is not a feature in your face but you have found the way to teach it some affected convulsion . . . and your language draws people's eyes upon the raree-show" (2.1.60–70). For this character, it is Lady Fancyfull's artifice and affectation together that have made her ridiculous, literally turning her into a spectacle. Like what the late seventeenth century called wit, her body's "language" is unnatural; it is unnecessarily learned, and destructively so. She has "taught" her face "affected convulsions," and her "language," by "drawing" people's eyes to view her "raree show,""unnaturally" turns her very existence into a theatrical production. Her "composition," like Vanbrugh's drama (and architecture), is thought to suffer from an excess of rhetorical flourish.

In the last act Lady Fancyfull achieves her greatest rhetorical flourish. Trying to rewrite the ending, she shows up at a wedding and delivers notes to the bride and groom, each note suggesting that the other partner is already married. She is foiled in her attempt. But because the plot could have proceeded to a marriage without Fancyfull's plan and, when her attempt is foiled, does so anyway, the attempt constitutes, characteristically, an embellishment within the finished play. Thus, this parlorroom intrigue is a clever addition, extraneous to the structure of the play, from an "impertinent composition" who specializes in "teaching""affected convulsions."

It is important that Lady Fancyfull's failed attempt at rewriting the ending is described in terms of the Fall (especially considering how Jeremy Collier responded to what he called "the immorality and profaneness" of Vanbrugh's plays). Asked "who 'tis has put you upon all this mischief," a servant involved replies, "Satan and his equipage." Exclaiming "as fell Adam, so fell I," the servant refers to his lover as his "Eve" (5.5.192–97), but, referring to Lady Fancyfull, he argues, "This is the serpent that tempted the woman" (5.5.204–5). Here, as in Milton's version, language is again at issue in the Fall. In *Paradise Lost* language affects Adam and

Eve's capacity to understand Raphael's narration, whereas in *The Provok'd Wife* Adam and Eve are instead tempted to rewrite the story, to effect a different ending.

Lady Fancyfull's failed attempt to write the ending of the story and her sense earlier that writing and letting it alone are the same thing are mirrored in Vanbrugh's similarly failed attempt to complete the play as a whole. *The Provok'd Wife* ends with an "epilogue" which complains about the play's lack of an epilogue: "No epilogue? / I swear I know of none. / Lord! How shall we excuse it to the town? / Why, we must e'en say something of our own" (1–3). In this way the play diffuses the authority of the author, or as Lady Brute notes in the erstwhile epilogue, "We speak not from the poet now" (12). In the end, there is almost no ending, and because the author supposedly has failed to write one, the epilogue is just an improvisation concocted by the characters or actors. Vanbrugh has willfully failed to fulfill the expectations placed on him either by the rules or by the town.

Collier's *Short View of the Immorality and Profaneness of the English Stage*, in which he criticizes several recent plays, both of Vanbrugh's among them, unself-consciously mimics the treatment of Lady Fancyfull by the characters of *The Provok'd Wife*. Although Collier concedes that "the English Stage has always been out of Order," Vanbrugh's play persuades him that it has "never [been out of Order] to the Degree 'tis at present." Like Lady Fancyfull, contemporary plays "appear a Heap of Irregularities," unruly. Collier makes the central claim for the rules, that "the Design of these Rules [the "*Three Unities* of Time, Place and Action"] is . . . to make the Play appear more Natural." The rules facilitate imitation of the regularity and clarity of what Collier considers natural distinctions. Behind his argument about the efficacy of the rules, Collier assumes that "the Lines of Virtue and Vice are Struck out by Nature in very Legible Distinctions."[10] For Collier the rules work because of what he presumes to be the clarity of the natural distinction between vice and virtue; they already correspond to these "Lines" in nature. Collier's argument here is reminiscent of Heartfree's in *The Provok'd Wife*: Lady Fancyfull has been "ungrateful" to "nature," having "undone [it] by art" (2.1.55, 58, 60).

The potential consequences of Collier's position that ethical distinctions are "Natural" can be seen in his claim that modesty is "proportion'd" into women.[11] Lady Brute's decision, despite the circumstances under which it was made, is consequently irregular, unnatural, and ultimately wrong, because it goes against the "proportion'd" modesty he contends has been naturally built into every woman. It is important here that Collier should invoke proportion, a term of classical architecture. On one level, it is a formal point with political implications; what would seem to be a point about ethical appropriateness has been cast in mathematical, and maybe even spatial, terms. On another level, it shows that in a sense architecture is at issue in Collier's argument.

Although it might seem that he is referring solely to the dramatic rules, Collier himself indicates an architectural understanding of them. He claims that "if Virtue has no Prospect, 'tis not worth owning," in which case virtue is a house which requires a good view in order for it to be valuable real estate. If virtue is a house, then Collier would argue that it be built according to the classical rules of architecture. Collier's description of Vanbrugh's *The Relapse* as "an ill-proportion'd rant, without warrant in Nature or Antiquity," draws on the classical intersection of the architectural and the mathematical in the idea of proportion.[12] Interestingly enough, Collier combines this term with a more explicitly political assumption that a play should require a "warrant." We might say that for Collier, it is the rules that provide a play with a license to imitate.

Vanbrugh, in response, concedes that he might not "have observed the strictest Prescriptions" but argues that "the Rules fall as short of the disorders of the Mind, as those of the Physicians do in the Diseases of the Body; and I think a man may vary from 'em both without being a quack in either."[13] Admitting the disorder that Collier criticizes, Vanbrugh claims that his disorderly plays accurately represent a natural, human disorderliness. Because of his attempt to achieve this kind of realism, Vanbrugh's plays do not follow the rules; his plays do not follow the rules because people do not follow them. A strict adherence to the rules would prohibit what might be called the excesses requisite for an effective characterization of the real. Although *realism* and *naturalism* are terms vexed well beyond the scope of this chapter, by relying as much as possible on how Collier and Vanbrugh here use such words, it can be said provisionally that the terms refer to a set of changing, historically specific conventions that create what is then thought to be a lifelike illusion. Such conventions change, frequently because other conventions begin to feel confining or stilted. In the case of Vanbrugh and Collier, we are looking at the record of a moment in which Vanbrugh's practice is placing pressure on a previous understanding of naturalistic illusion. Vanbrugh stakes his claim for variety, for varying from the rules, by suggesting that such variety might be more realistic, more natural, by virtue of its ability to capture the exceptional.

The Provok'd Wife itself discusses the possibility of a discrepancy between the reasonable and the natural, casting such a discussion, interestingly enough, as a dialogue between Lady Fancyfull and her servant, who is French (probably not coincidentally, given the dialogue's topic). Wondering whether "reason corrects Nature," Lady Fancyfull asks Mademoiselle, "Do you then prefer your nature to your reason?" (1.2.159, 161). Mademoiselle says she does, "because my nature makes me merry, my reason make me mad" (1.2.165). Unlike what we have seen as Alberti's, Wotton's, or Milton's understanding of a universal correlation between nature and reason, *The Provok'd Wife* here playfully suggests a discrepancy between the two. When Mademoiselle lists a series of physical needs— "eat," "drink," "sleep," and "live"—and claims "de nature bid you do one, de nature bid you do toder" (1.2.156–58), she is suggesting that even natural

impulses can pull in contradictory, and therefore occasionally unreasonable, directions. This dialogue indicates a tension between what reason
and nature would "bid," a tension that animates not only Lady Fancyfull's
character in the play but, by extension, Vanbrugh as author and architect.

Vanbrugh's defense of his play might be summarized with the question he puts to readers of his *Vindication*: "The real Query is, whether the
way I have varied, be likely to have a good Effect, or a bad one?"[14] That
same question applies to Vanbrugh's architecture as well, including his
design for his theater. He has varied from the rules in both his play and
his theater, or as he explains, he has not "observed the strictest Prescriptions."

Vanbrugh's Queen's/Haymarket Theatre, more explicitly than *The
Provok'd Wife*, had its politics inscribed into its foundations: the corner-
stone was engraved with the phrase "the little Whig."[15] As was also the
case with the play, the building's express political affiliation presents it
with a formal problem. On the one hand, if this Whiggish political affiliation is foundational for Vanbrugh, then a theater in the grand tradition
by the implicit grandeur of its formal associations is part of a political
argument. But on the other hand, a mere assertion of the greatness of a
formal lineage would run counter to the Whiggish political innovation;
politically, it is the Stuarts who represent formal lineage. Consequently,
as is characteristic of the author who is represented by Lady Fancyfull or
of the author of a *Vindication* in which he claims he feels little need to justify, Vanbrugh made several architectural decisions that counter what he
calls "the too exact observance of the Rules," or as he notes in a letter to
Jacob Tonson: "I have drawn a design for the whole disposition of the
inside, very different from any Other House in being."[16] In this theater,
as in his plays, he avoided the too strict observance of the rules. Perhaps
too much so. Within three years of opening, its interior needed to be
renovated.

In his 13 July 1703 letter to Tonson, Vanbrugh describes the lot on

which the theater would stand, "the second Stable Yard going up to the
Haymarket."[17] The theater's site occasioned much sarcastic treatment: an
anonymous pamphlet was astounded that Vanbrugh could achieve the
Herculean feat of "Transform[ing] a Stable into a Theater."[18] In an issue of
the Review devoted entirely to the opening of Vanbrugh's new theater,
Defoe wrote a satirical, scatological poem in which he delicately points
out

> A Lay-stall this, Apollo spoke the Word,
> And straight arose a Playhouse from a T[urd]. . . .
> Some call this Metamorphosis a Jest,
> And say, we're but a Dunghill still at best.[19]

According to his 1703 letter, Vanbrugh was able to acquire the stable's
land for £2,000. He had "lay'd up such a Scheme of matters, that I shall
be reimburs'd every penny of it but," he explains, "this is a Secret lest they
shou'd lay hold on't, to lower the Rent."[20]

After describing his secret plan for purchasing the land and the originality of his theater's design, Vanbrugh asks Tonson to purchase an
architectural textbook for him: "The book you mention wch I wanted,
you'll oblige me to get. 'Tis Palladio in French." Here, his Lady Fancyfull–like admission that he has drawn a design for the theater "very different from any Other House in being," preceding as it does his request
for a book on architecture, makes it seem that Vanbrugh designed buildings first and read about architecture later. However, the fact that Vanbrugh knew about Palladio—and different editions of Palladio at that—
suggests that by 1703 Vanbrugh was not entirely unschooled in
architecture.[21]

Vanbrugh's request for Palladio in connection with his theater indicates that he saw the Haymarket as following a line of Renaissance theater design which begins with Palladio's Teatro Olimpico in Vicenza (a
possibility which is further supported by the form of the interior of the

Haymarket's Theater). "The first permanent indoor theater of the Renaissance," the Teatro Olimpico was designed and begun by Palladio in 1580 and completed by Scamozzi in 1585.[22] Like Palladio's illustration of a "Roman Theater" in Daniele Barbaro's edition of Vitruvius (1556), the Teatro Olimpico features an elliptical arrangement of tiered benches for audience seating (fig. 2).

This semicircular seating arrangement was to prove extraordinarily influential for seventeenth-century British architects. When Inigo Jones traveled to Italy in 1613–14, he visited Vicenza, where he may also have visited the Teatro Olimpico.[23] Upon returning to England, Jones

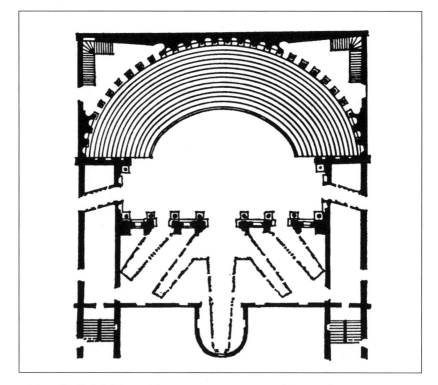

2. Plan of Palladio's Teatro Olimpico, Vicenza, 1580–85. (From Ludwig H. Heydenreich and Wolfgang Lotz, *Architecture in Italy*, 1400–1600 [Harmondsworth: Penguin, 1974], courtesy of Yale University Press Pelican History of Art)

designed a theater, the Cockpit-in-Court (fig. 3), which with its octagonal shape seems to have grafted Palladio's theater onto what was then the governing linear English model, giving the theater an angular, octagonal plan rather than the Palladian semicircle. Generally, the revived theater of the Restoration had to make do with such spaces as they could find; often, these spaces had previously been used as tennis courts.[24] According to Richard Leacroft, "The limitations of the existing forms of the rectangular tennis courts necessarily imposed their own pattern."[25] As a consequence, these Restoration theaters were long, rectangular boxes with seating on straight benches parallel with the front of the stage. Both

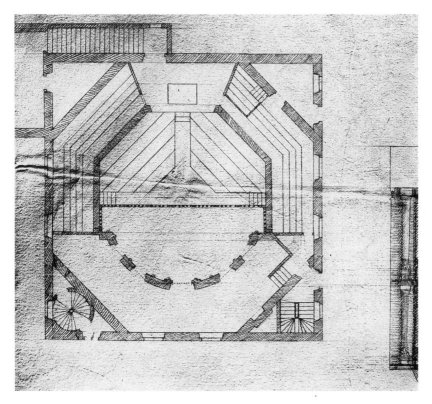

3. Inigo Jones, Cockpit-in-Court Theatre. (Courtesy of The Provost and Fellows of Worcester College, Oxford)

the Vere Street Theatre (1660) and the Lincoln's Inn's Fields Theatre
(1661) were designed in this way, as was, at least on the orchestra level, the
Dorset Garden Theatre, built ten years later (1671).

By drawing, as Inigo Jones did, on the elliptical Palladian theater,
Christopher Wren's theater designs stood out from their Restoration
contemporaries. Unlike the rectangular tennis-court theater of the
Restoration, with straight pew-style seating, Wren's Sheldonian (1663)

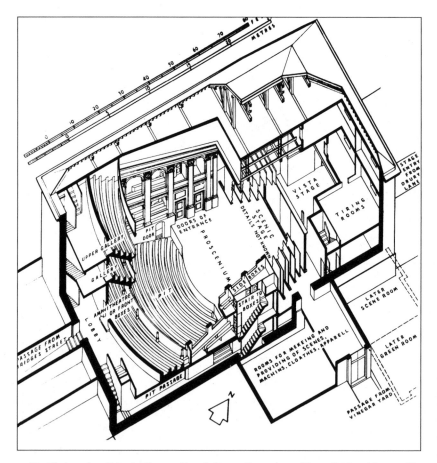

4. Sir Christopher Wren's Theatre Royal, Drury Lane, 1674. (From Richard Leacroft's
Development of the English Playhouse [London: Methuen, 1971], courtesy of Random
House)

and Royal Drury Lane Theatres (1674) have the Palladian semicircular
shape (fig. 4). Drury Lane also features ornamental columns on the side
walls, which signal the theater's classical affiliations and also fit a certain
vision of how an audience and a theater should focus on a stage drama;
Wren designed them "in perspective, reducing in height as it nears the
scenic area."[26]

Vanbrugh's Haymarket Theatre, which opened in 1705, falls into the
tradition of theater architecture that began with Palladio in Italy and
continued with Inigo Jones and Sir Christopher Wren in England. Vanbrugh's theater featured a circular form derived stylistically from Palla-

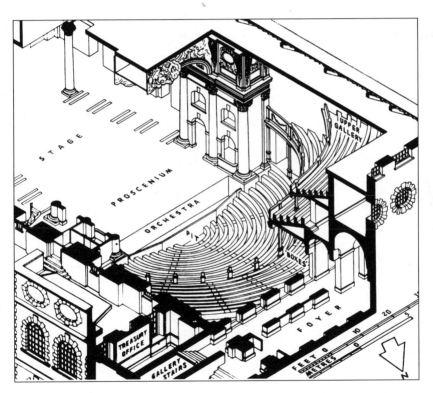

5. Sir John Vanbrugh, Queen's/Haymarket Theatre, 1705. (From Richard Leacroft,
Development of the English Playhouse [London: Methuen, 1973], courtesy of Random
House)

dio, i.e., the orchestra seating was arranged in a semicircle. And like Wren at Drury Lane, Vanbrugh placed three "giant Corinthian columns" along each of the theater's interior side walls.[27] These elements aligned his new theater with the very best that classical theater architecture had to offer (fig. 5).

However, where Wren had arranged the columns for perspectival effect, Vanbrugh placed his columns parallel to one another, like a box, rather than in Wren's fan shape. This box created for the columns prevented viewers on the edges of the semicircular seating from seeing the stage. In other words, Vanbrugh's theater was not a good place in which actually to see a production. Colley Cibber is highly critical of it: "Almost every proper Quality and Convenience of a good Theater had been sacrificed or neglected to show the Spectator a vast triumphal piece of Architecture!" Vanbrugh's Haymarket Theatre was affected by what we might call its Lady Fancyfull quality. Cibber's response to it—"extraordinary and superfluous"; "What could [the] vast [ness], [the] gild[ing], [the] immoderat[ion] avail?"—is reminiscent of how characters in The Provok'd Wife complain about Lady Fancyfull: in both cases an impertinent composition places art before nature, generating "affected convulsions." The perception of an extraordinary and superfluous quality, attributed to Lady Fancyfull in The Provok'd Wife and to the details of Vanbrugh's Haymarket Theatre, stayed with Vanbrugh throughout his career as an architect.

Cibber goes on to say that the acoustics were as bad as the sight lines, if not worse. The Haymarket, like most eighteenth-century theaters, had a stage which thrust into the audience, providing the actors a defined space where they could step forward and deliver their lines. But Vanbrugh put a dome—peaking fifteen feet higher than the cornice—directly over the stage. Consequently, as Cibber tells us, "this extraordinary and superfluous Space occasion'd such an Undulation, from the Voice of every Actor, that the articulate sounds of a speaking voice were drowned by the hollow reverberations of one word upon another."[28] By December 1705, eight months after the theater had opened, Congreve had dropped out of the company, complaining that he had been "dipt."[29] Almost fifteen years later Vanbrugh wrote to Jacob Tonson, confiding that "I have no money to dispose of. I have been many years at hard Labour, to work through the Cruel Difficultys, that Haymarket involv'd me in. . . . Nor are those difficultys, quite at an end yet."[30]

In some ways Vanburgh's position within late seventeenth- and early eighteenth-century British classicism is similar to Claude Perrault's contemporary argument with French classicism. Commissioned by Colbert in 1664 to work on a translation of and a commentary on Vitruvius, Claude Perrault published an *Ordonnance des cinq espèces de colonnes selon la méthode des anciens* (1683), in which he undermines the mathematical, universal understanding of Vitruvian architectural theory. Perrault points out that if music is going to be considered as an analogy for architecture, then it is important to take into account cultural differences in music: the way "harmonies" are applied "differs with different musicians and countries, just as the application of architectural proportions differs with different authors and buildings." Although the basis for his claim may differ from Vanbrugh's, arguing that "pleasing variation can sometimes give rise to a perfect . . . beauty without strict adherence to any proportional rule" is as unusual in a late seventeenth-century context as Vanbrugh's argument that "a man may vary . . . without being a quack."[31] Not only was this attitude of Vanbrugh's, defending variation, an important way of figuring a Whiggish vision of the immediate post-1688 settlement, it would also be very influential during what is considered the early Gothic Revival.

It would be disingenuous not to wonder how Vanbrugh got the chance to make his Whiggish argument, either in literature or in architecture. Vanbrugh's first mention of the Haymarket Theatre, in his July 1703 letter to Jacob Tonson, then living in Amsterdam, begins with a remarkably bawdy description of Lord Halifax, Congreve, and Vanbrugh "sopping our Arses in the fountain" at Hampton Court.[32] The rakish privilege suggested by such an image is double-edged. The three seem like fools; but they are incredibly lucky fools, acting foolish in remarkably pleasant surroundings. One cannot help but wonder whether such familiar access fuels either Vanbrugh's little need to justify (architecturally and ethically) or his extraordinarily quick rise to architectural prominence. It is probably scenes such as this which prompt Kerry Downes to state, "Our knowledge of how Vanbrugh won Castle Howard . . . [is] still sketchy and the fact of it barely credible. Either Vanbrugh was in 1699 an amateur without training or experience, or he was not. If he was, his assets can only have been imagination, a natural eye, good friends, and remarkable, not to say excessive, self-confidence."[33] Of course, most famously in the case of Sir Christopher Wren (who was Savilian Professor of Astronomy before and after he suddenly became an architect by designing the Sheldonian Theatre), the line between amateur and professional architect was not so rigid in the seventeenth and eighteenth centuries. But the Hampton Court passage from the 1703 letter does say a lot about what Downes calls Vanbrugh's "good friends." Not every amateur was lucky enough to get the prestigious commissions Vanbrugh would go on to receive, especially that of Blenheim Palace.

In the process of building Blenheim Palace, Vanbrugh and the duchess of Marlborough famously argue in their correspondence about his vision for it, repeating the themes, and occasionally the terms, of the previous discussions of his play and theater.[34] As far as the duchess is concerned, Vanbrugh, like Lady Fancyfull, is designing what characters in *The Provok'd Wife* call an "impertinent composition." In fact, in her dismissive treatment of Vanbrugh's idea, the duchess uses the same language that Heartfree used in his critique of Lady Fancyfull: "some ridiculous air or other"[35] (2.1.68). In this well-recorded disagreement the duchess of Malborough traditionally is remembered as the "Wicked

Woman of Marl," as Vanbrugh referred to her, but it is often overlooked that she was a builder and architect herself, having designed an almshouse and two important park buildings, not to mention supervising the construction of four new houses. Her insistence on a "strong, useful, and plain" architecture represented an informed opposition to Vanbrugh's approach.[36] Yet try as the duchess might, she could not implement her vision for Blenheim Palace; Vanbrugh was able to make the argument for what she called "the madnesses of it."[37] A little later in the eighteenth century, she might have had more luck; architect, architectural patron, and architectural publisher Lord Burlington, for example, was "very much inclined to dislike everything there."

3

"The Utmost Grace of Uniformity": Pope's Anglo-Palladian Epic

✍ UPON FIRST VISITING VANBRUGH'S Blenheim Palace, Alexander Pope wrote, "I never saw so great a thing with so much littleness in it." Such a complaint, in itself, was by no means unusual, but not everyone who complained about Blenheim also designed their own home, sketched interior improvements for their friends' homes, or wrote some of the most important English poetry of the first half of the eighteenth century. Pope's contention that "some trifling littleness . . . every where destroy[s] the grandeur" of Blenheim suggests his interest in and response to architecture and offers a way of considering Pope's formal preferences generally.[1] Apparently, the way in which Vanbrugh "varies" from the rules was not an option that Pope was willing to consider for his own work. The terms of his critique of Blenheim, focusing on what he calls "littleness," suggest that he would prefer something more closely focused on the massing, considered as a whole, something smoother or more uniform.

Pope's disagreement with Vanbrugh's version of classicism acquires additional importance when we consider that Milton's *Paradise Lost* also would not suffice for Pope, who once told Joseph Spence that "Milton's style in *Paradise Lost* is not natural."[2] With both Vanbrugh's varying from the rules and Milton's Vitruvian structure excluded, Pope is left with the challenge of finding a formal approach that would seem "natural" in his own terms. Pope's claim—that he must find "something domestic, fit for my own country, and for my own time"—indicates that there are nationalist and generational reasons why neither Milton's nor Vanbrugh's styles would suit him.[3] The "domestic" style that Pope must find will of necessity have to be different from theirs.

In architectural terms, Pope had available to him a contemporary model thought to represent the classical, the natural, and the "domestic": the Palladian idea of the villa. As much a genre—an accumulation of patterned and repeated formulaic tropes "rooted in the contrast of country and city"—as it is an actual building, the villa is historically comprised of two building types—"the self-sustaining agricultural estate [and] the villa . . . conceived primarily as a retreat."[4] Pope's villa, Twickenham, in the Thames Valley, "the real home of the English villa," combined both; he could not have built it without the money he made from sales of his translations (the relatively urban market from which he could retreat), but he also prided himself on the productivity of Twickenham's gardens: "I am now my own master too much; my house is too large; my gardens furnish too much wood and provision for my use."[5] As Helen Deutsch reminds us, however, such claims about retirement "ignore the socio-economic links between the city and the country."[6]

The terms of Pope's appreciation for Lord Digby's estate at Sherborne draw on the idea of the villa and echo opposition themes: "I cannot make the reflection I've often done upon contemplating the beautiful Villas of Other Noblemen, rais'd upon the Spoils of plunder'd nations, or aggrandiz'd by the wealth of the Publick. I cannot ask myself

the question, 'What Else has this man to be liked? What else has he cultivated or improv'd? What good, or what desirable thing appears of him,
without these walls?'"[7] Pope believed that the villa should be part of a
benevolent political arrangement, contributing to the civic life of its area.
In this he was not alone, for the villa was seen as a powerful political
alternative. If the City, especially in the early eighteenth century, began to
look politically like the Court once did, then the alternative political culture, the political culture independent of or disinterested in the City,
could develop around the villa, outside the City, without quite being in
the country. Regarding his own villa, Twickenham, Pope claims that "my
house is like the house of a Patriarch of old, standing by the highway side
and receiving all travelers."[8] Standing by the highway—in other words,
outside or, more importantly, perhaps between cities—the villa owner
dispenses patriarchal generosity.

From what James Ackerman calls the ideology of the villa, Pope
gleaned the possibility of demonstrating a kind of independence, both
religious and political. Because of its comparatively modest scale and its
potential for agricultural self-sufficiency, "the villa was perceived as one
instrument by which the middle class might emulate and challenge the
privilege of the aristocracy and gentry."[9] In the same way that the seventeenth-century "Country Seat . . . was the physical manifestation of complex political and economic theory and policy, one which belonged to a
definite historical period," so too was the early eighteenth-century "Palladian" villa a historical manifestation of a complex political theory. They
may have been more expensive and more landed than what many people
lived in, but villas such as Twickenham or Marble Hill House were
smaller than "prodigy houses" such as Blenheim Palace or Houghton
Hall; the decision to build one created the impression of separation from
court politics.[10]

Pope claims that he wants to protect the idea of independence generally and the reputation of his own independence specifically: "Courts I

see not, Courtiers I know not, Kings I adore not, Queens I compliment not; so am never like to be in fashion, nor in dependence" (2:469). "As a Catholic, forbidden by law from owning land," and as someone who wanted to participate in the public life of early eighteenth-century Britain, Pope has important social and political reasons for wanting to seem independent, or disinterested, and his correspondence often shows his disinterest: "Do not think I have any interested aim in this Advice."[11] Concerned, for example, about the fact that "some call . . . me a Papist and a Tory . . . Others . . . a Whig," Pope responds that it would be a "much more natural" conclusion "to think a person who has been favored by all sides has been inoffensive to all."[12] Here Pope is making a new claim about what it means to be "natural"; unlike either Milton or Vanbrugh, Pope believes not only that it is possible to be "inoffensive," but that it is more "natural" as well.

The *Essay on Man* embodies this disinterested, "inoffensive," and consequently "natural" theory of independence; Pope says so himself when he writes to the earl of Oxford, stating that *An Essay on Man* "will consist of nothing but such doctrines as are inoffensive."[13] Although he might be "ambitious of nothing but the good opinion of all men of all sides,"[14] at first glance Pope's proposal to write an "inoffensive" poem would seem impossible. And yet, despite the difficulties implicit such a project, we have *An Essay on Man*, so successful in its inoffensiveness that it is occasionally offensive—most famously of course in what Laura Brown calls "Pope's least respected line: 'One truth is clear, Whatever IS, is RIGHT.'"[15] As was immediately recognized, too much is wrong for all to be "RIGHT." Or as Kevin Cope has wryly suggested, "Pope, in the last analysis, has more in common with Dulness than anyone would like to admit."[16]

But this "dulness" constitutes part of Pope's strategy of independence, disinterestedness, and inoffensiveness, and these qualities are all part of what Pope's work offers to the early eighteenth century. Like Shaftesbury, as described by Lawrence Klein, "the argument at the heart of [Pope's] cultural politics was that, while the Church and the Court had traditionally dominated English culture to its detriment, post-1688 and post-1707 Britain had the opportunity to create a new public."[17] In the neo-Palladian architectural revival, such disinterestedness seemed possible through the form or idea of the villa; in Pope's neo-Palladian *Essay on Man*, it seemed possible in the form or idea of the letter, the epistle. In fact, the two are related, at least in Pope's work: in both cases, a republican self-sufficiency and a simultaneous participation in a highly sociable lifestyle, by widening the circle of visiting friends (or broadening the reading audience), offered a standardization—a "methodization"—of political (and cultural) life which could re-create a national community then thought to have been lost in the upheavals of the seventeenth century. It is what J. G. A. Pocock calls "a politics of style accompanied by a morality of politeness."[18] In light of Pope's interest and participation in contemporary architecture, the *Essay on Man* constitutes an Anglo-Palladian epic—an epic of disinterestedness—which, like the Palladian architectural revival, offers what Pope might call disinterestedness as a political model.

This chapter, in establishing the terms and extent of Pope's participation in architecture, takes its cue to some extent from Pope himself, who wrote to Swift in 1732 that his "works will in one respect be like the works of Nature, much more to be liked and understood when consider'd in the relation they bear with each other."[19] It assumes that Pope's "works" as author and as architect should be seen in the relation they bear to one another, a relation which is then used to discuss the form of *An Essay on Man*. In focusing on early eighteenth-century questions regarding literary and architectural form, this chapter explores reasons behind what Pat Rogers calls Pope's "odd ambition"—"to introduce a new 'correctness' to English poetry."[20] It should be noted that Pope was not alone among early eighteenth-century writers in advocating formal

correctness. Shaftesbury and Hutcheson, for instance, are similarly insis-
tent that "the figures [which] excite in us the ideas of beauty seem to be
those in which there is *uniformity amidst variety*," as Hutcheson claims.[21]
Such similar understandings of form from other early eighteenth-century authors suggest that Pope was participating in a larger discussion
about the importance of formal correctness, an argument amply illustrated in the architectural theory of the day.

Distinguished by an almost obsessive search for formal simplicity,
meaning both the supposed simplicity of life in the villa and the formal
arrangement of its architectural elements, early eighteenth-century
British architectural theory focused on Palladio, whose villas, arranged
around a central vertical axis, on either side of which the rooms "strictly
reflect each other," simplified symmetry. In early eighteenth-century England, Palladio was not Palladio the builder and was only sometimes Palladio the author of the *Four Books*; for the neo-Palladian revival, "Palladio"
and Palladianism ultimately constituted metonymies for simplifying and
standardizing. Palladio, write Hersey and Freedman, "was part of the
movement that deprived the word [*symmetry*] of its earlier meaning and
gave it its modern one."[22] If for Vitruvius *analogia* denotes what is today
called proportion, and for Alberti "harmony" entails the musical possibilities Alberti seems to invite self-consciously, then Palladio's contribution
was to reinterpret these rational architectural terms into what we today
call symmetry, understood principally as reflection on either side of an
axis. At the same time, it was not lost on early eighteenth-century
observers that in Palladio's villas the placement of the living quarters and
the farm buildings "emphasized the formal separation of the two
domains, which were not to compete against each other in their aesthetic
claims, despite their mutual unity."[23] With Palladio, even what was
brought together was kept apart, and symmetry was one way of achieving this unified separation.

Pope was personally involved in the British neo-Palladian reconsideration of architecture. In 1716, when Pope's family moved to Chiswick, "the center of the burgeoning English Palladian movement," he became neighbor and friend to Richard Boyle, third earl of Burlington, who acquired a substantial collection of original Palladio drawings, subscribed to and published several important neo-Palladian architectural publications, and whose house at Chiswick, ostensibly designed in imitation of Palladio's Rotonda, was a flagship of the British neo-Palladian revival.[24] Pope gained a personal introduction to the Palladian architects, architecture, and architecture patrons, including the duke of Argyll, Lord Bathurst, Lord Bolingbroke, the earl of Burlington, Colen Campbell, James Gibbs, and the earl of Oxford, people who were shaping the architectural program of their day (and who reshaped the landscape of England).

In 1719, on the back of the manuscript of his translation of Homer, Pope drew the elevation and the plan of what looks like the façade of his future home—Twickenham—featuring a tripartite pedimented façade

6. Sketch of house front and interior from Pope's Homer manuscript. (By permission of The British Library, Add MS 4809 f.84v)

with a portico on the upper story (figs. 6, 7). Pope combines a cube with a temple-style pedimented colonnade in the middle of which is set the so-called Palladian window. These drawings, featuring as they do a building with the typically Palladian tripartite elevation, show that Pope was familiar with and influenced by the received Palladian style. But more importantly, they also show that literature and architecture constituted for Pope quite literally two sides of the same page; on one side of the sheet he is translating Homer, on the other making architectural sketches.

Pope's reputation as an architect grew among his friends, so much so that in some of his letters he provides architectural advice. For example, in a 1731 letter to Fortescue, Pope writes:

> As to your Building, I heartily wish you had sent me a plan of it, in which I might possibly be of more Service to you than by barely sending you the Proportions you desire. It is not easy to answer your question of

7. Sketch of a Palladian building from Pope's Homer manuscript. (By permission of The British Library, Add MS 4809 f.84v)

the Doors & Windows, the Dimension of them being to b[e] suited to
the Size & Height of the Room, which you do not tell me. But in general
both Doors and Windows should be a double Square, & the solid of the
walls between Window & Window rather more than the Opening: no
harm in exceeding in the Solids to near twice the dimension of the windows. If the Windows be large (above 3 foot abroad) the Doors need be
no larger; but if the Windows be less, make the doors rather above three
feet wide: the height just double to whatever your width.[25]

Besides indicating that Pope's friends trusted him as a source of architectural information, this passage also suggests the degree to which
Pope's understanding of architecture relied on classical architectural
writings; there is, for example, a similar passage in Sir Henry Wotton's
book (a work with which we know Pope was familiar, as Pope mentions
Wotton in his conversations with Joseph Spence).[26] In the letter to
Fortescue, Pope refers to proportion and goes into remarkable detail
concerning the appropriate proportions for a door: they should be suited
to the size of a room, and in general a double square. Windows should
also be a double square, but the ratio between windows should be more
than the width of one window, although there is no harm in having the
walls between windows almost equal to the window widths.

In another context Pope claims that "there is a certain Majesty in
Simplicity."[27] Although on the one hand, Pope's interest in simplicity is
part of the early eighteenth-century reconsideration of classicism, on the
other, the fact that Pope also refers to "a certain Majesty" reveals an
important corollary of British neo-Palladian simplicity: politics. For
example, James Gibbs, with whom Pope worked on redesigning his
Twickenham home, claims in the title of his 1732 book that he can provide *Rules for Drawing . . . in a more exact and easy manner . . . by which all
FRACTIONS . . . are avoided.* It is one thing to offer a method of architectural drawing which avoids fractions, but it is another thing to claim

doing so will be "more exact." Using fewer fractions may make something more simple, but it will also make it less exact. Gibbs seems to confuse simplicity and exactness, but this exacting avoidance of fractions is consistent with an implication throughout several of the Palladian publications.

In that both could be said to represent division, Gibbs's Palladian "fractions" figuratively describe political factions, and Palladianism held out the possibility of creating a more uniformly proportioned community that moved beyond fractions. Most explicit in this regard is Robert Morris, who argues for an architecture in which "beautiful and harmonious Productions aris[e] from . . . the agreeable Symmetry and Concordance of every particular separate Member, centred and united on the oeconomy of the Whole . . . regulated . . . in a due Proportion."[28] Although Morris's argument replays the terms of Vitruvian classicism—"harmonious," "Symmetry," "Concordance," and "Proportion"—he significantly adds "the oeconomy as a whole." This version of classicism shifts the focus to the economy, using symmetry as a claim for the appropriate way to organize civil society. To this extent, then, what is called Palladianism participates in the early eighteenth-century discussion of what J. G. A. Pocock calls the "the ideological importance of secular culture." The Palladian theory of the simplified and the uniform, "centred and united on the oeconomy of the Whole," overlaps with what Christine Gerrard describes as "a civic-humanist tradition of Commonwealth thought and argument."[29]

Although An Essay on Man's dedication to Bolingbroke already indicates its oppositional affiliation, my interest in relating Pope's poem to theories of the Palladian revival is to investigate why this oppositional poem takes the form that it does. The Essay on Man here is understood to have been placed in a relationship with the subject of my first chapter, Milton's Paradise Lost. In itself, this is not a new claim; according to Dustin Griffin, "that An Essay on Man prominently alludes to Paradise

Lost, invites comparison with it, and even may be said to be a 'transliteration' of Milton's themes into 'rationalistic terms' have become established truths about the poem since Maynard Mack's Twickenham edition thirty-five years ago."[30] This chapter does not aim to overturn the perception of a connection between the two poems; instead, I use early eighteenth-century architectural theory to offer an explanation for some of the many significant differences between the two poems. If the connections between *Paradise Lost* and *Essay on Man* are so obvious, then why does Pope's poem emerge so different from that of Milton? Why, as Margaret Doody puts it, should "the tone, the idiom [and] . . . the style have changed"?[31] Perhaps such a change is due in part to the early eighteenth-century British Palladian revival's emphasis on a methodical simplicity, offering what Pope calls "Nature Methodiz'd," a filter through which *Essay on Man* could reread *Paradise Lost*.[32]

The differences between Milton, Vanbrugh, and Pope can be seen in the ways they each handle the question of what Milton calls "justification." Milton sets out to "justify the ways of God to men" (*Paradise Lost* 1.26), Vanbrugh claims "I need trouble myself . . . little to justify," and in the *Essay on Man*, Pope tries to "vindicate the ways of God to Man" (1.16).[33] Milton's "justification," Vanbrugh's lack of it, and Pope's "vindication," besides representing different ethical positions, also entail different aesthetic attitudes. Each position is self-confident in its own way. Milton argues that God's ways can be shown to be reasonable, and Vanbrugh contends that his work can stand for itself with no other defense, even though it is being so famously and seemingly successfully criticized. But a poet who believes that God can be vindicated is making a particular, and different, claim. To vindicate is to be more convincing than to justify; vindication carries with it the strength of conviction that avenging requires. Pope's *Essay on Man* claims to have that conviction: "One truth is clear, Whatever IS, is RIGHT" (1.294).[34] If Milton's style, in its attempt to justify, is not "natural," and Vanbrugh's, in its avoidance of justification,

has too much "littleness," then Pope needs to find a form—or what he
calls a "style"—which can convey the poem's sense of truth's clarity
(rather than its complexity).

Formally, or rhetorically, the two most obvious differences between
Milton's *Paradise Lost* and Pope's *An Essay on Man* are Pope's use of the letter and of the rhyming couplet, both of which are related to Pope's Palladian notion of what constitutes the "natural." According to Pope, letters
have a generic claim to what he calls, in a letter to Lady Mary Wortley
Montagu, the "artless & natural,"[35] upon which he relies both in his *Correspondence* and *An Essay on Man*. In his *Correspondence* he throws "myself
upon paper,"[36] there is nothing he "would not, in my own nature, declare
to all mankind,"[37] and his letters "will be the most impartial Representa-
tions of a free heart."[38] Of course, even Pope himself would admit that
these declarations of natural epistolary honesty are merely rhetorical
devices (witness his wish to edit his own collected letters), but the
generic presumption of informality that accompanies the epistle is
important for Pope's poetry of the 1730s.

The letter automatically implies an audience, a person to whom the
letter has been written. As William Dowling explains, Pope's epistolary
poem thus becomes "an over-hearing or listening in on the exchange
between letter-writer and addressee," represented, in the case of *An Essay
on Man*, by Pope addressing his friend Bolingbroke. The reader—by
noticing the poem's formal poetic qualities, which, as Dowling puts it,
"operate . . . to signal its status as public object"—can participate in the
private world usually indicated by the privacy of a letter.[39] In architectural terms, the reader can in a sense visit the private world of the Palladian villa at Twickenham. However, the epistolary style also implies a
particular type of relationship between writer and audience. Because it is
friendly, artless, and intimate, "in the letter, philosophy and rhetoric were
allowed to take leave of formality," creating the powerful impression of
"philosophy as advice," as Klein points out.[40] More than just the reader

participating in a putatively private world, the letter form also creates a newly intimate public world, in which people can write or speak freely, presumably without fear of "faction." For this new claim to a public sphere, the epistle "represents the ultimate act of methodizing nature and naturalizing method."[41]

In explaining the second obvious difference between *Paradise Lost* and *An Essay on Man*, the rhyming couplet, Pope again uses spatial imagery: "verse, and even rhyme," is a smaller, or as he puts it, "shorter," form. While Pope concedes that he "might have done [the same *Essay*] in prose," he chose verse because he "found I could express them [principles, maxims, or precepts] more *shortly* this way than in prose itself."[42] In case a reader might imagine that Pope means to emphasize the temporal implications of "shortly," he explains that "what is now published, is only to be considered as a *general Map* of MAN." A map, of course, represents specifically spatial arrangements, a point Pope further accentuates by referring to the poem's "marking out . . . *extent* . . . *limits*, and . . . *connection*." The rhyming couplet is shorter, especially when compared to Milton's blank verse form, which given its line length and its lack of end rhyme (not to mention the poem's overall length), is relatively capacious in comparison with Pope's rhyming couplets.

Voltaire reports that he asked Pope why Milton had not "rimé" in *Paradise Lost*, to which Pope retorted, "Because he could not."[43] Rather than Pope suggesting that Milton was not poetically or linguistically capable of rhyming, it would seem to be Pope's belief that rhyming would not have been a "natural" form for Milton, that historical conditions made rhyming unnatural for him. Conversely, Percival Stockdale reported that Lord Lyttelton once asked Pope why he had not translated Homer into blank verse (as Milton might have done), to which Pope responded that "he could translate it more easily into rhyme."[44] In the same way that Milton could not use rhyming couplets, Pope could not use blank verse; Pope could translate "more easily" into rhyme. Rhyme strikes Pope as more "natural" in the eighteenth century. Dustin Griffin argues that "to turn Milton's blank verse into couplets in the eighteenth century was implicitly to 'correct' the poem," and *An Essay on Man's* rhyming couplet form methodizes, in the neo-Palladian sense of the word, Milton's blank verse.[45]

Pope's decision to use rhyming couplets was then not merely a stylistic decision but also a historical, and to some extent then a political, one. Tillotson uses the phrase "closed couplet" to describe the form of *An Essay on Man's* rhyming couplet lines. The couplets are "closed" in the way the diction and rhyme scheme lead the reader from one line into the next while also holding lines together in pairs. As Tillotson puts it, "Two couplets form together one unit."[46] Pope's lines thus take up less space and, moreover, have the effect of avoiding faction, or of centering and uniting upon the economy of the whole. At the same time, however, because they rhyme, the line "endings" also lead to the following line, at least half of the time. In other words, they must not really effect closure; they can only imply it. In this sense, there is what Ralph Cohen calls a "relation between metrics and poetics": "the couplet came to function as a major strategy for illustrating the kinds of compromise that were possible."[47] It represents an idea of unification.

But the political possibility implicit in the unification of the rhyming couplet often had to do, again, with spatial relations. For example, in the first epistle, lines 17 through 20 end with the words "man below . . . we know . . . his station here . . . to which refer." For *An Essay on Man*, those endings are typical: they include both a kind of space and a kind of certainty. Man's station is here below, and that is what we know. One might say that, at the ends of Pope's lines, we all have what Pope would call our place. And the rhyming couplet ties it together: in *An Essay on Man's* Palladian terms, "the part relates to the whole" (3.21).

An Essay on Man, which entails a British neo-Palladian concern for symmetry, simplicity, and method, represents a Palladian version of Mil-

ton's *Paradise Lost*. The series of four relatively short rhyming couplet
verse epistles allows Pope to naturalize—which is to say methodize
or simplify—Milton's epic themes. For Pope, living in what Leopold
Damrosch calls a "post-epic world," the *Essay on Man* is the closest possible approximation of an epic poem available in an age of methodical Palladianism, an intralingual translation of Milton's *Paradise Lost*, "carrying
over" that earlier, daunting epic for a contemporary, simplifying taste.[48]
Consider, for example, Milton's "Satan" and Pope's "Pride," both of whom,
in attempting to change places, play similar narrative roles. In *Paradise
Lost* it was Satan who rushed into the skies, aiming at Eden, the blessed
abode. In *An Essay on Man*, Pride imagines it can turn the space of the
earth into the space of a house: "my foot-stool earth, my canopy the skies"
(1.140), thus disturbing both a moral and, significantly, a spatial order.
Despite their similar actions the two characters are very different in the
two poems. In *Paradise Lost*, Satan has a personality and acts like a very
persuasive human being. *An Essay on Man's* Pride, on the other hand, is a
comparatively abstract concept, and rather than making it human (as *Pil-
grim's Progress*, for example, would do with an abstract concept), Pope's
Essay on Man insists on its abstraction. As the example of "Pride" suggests, *An Essay on Man* is not a personal poem, despite the presumed
familiarity of its epistle form; to have an interiority could make it too
interested.

    An Essay on Man describes interest as self-love and makes a distinc-
tion between self-love and reason. As is consistent with his relationship
to Palladianism, Pope describes their difference spatially: "Self-love still
stronger, as its objects nigh; Reason's at distance, and in prospect lie"
(2.71–72). Reason occupies a privileged position, seeing things in
panorama or from a vista. As John Barrell points out, in *An Essay on Man*
"those who can comprehend the order of society and nature are the
observers of a prospect, in which others are merely objects."[49] *An Essay on
Man's* narrator is such an observer. The preface, for example, contends

that "more good will accrue . . . by attending to the large, open and more perceptible parts, than by studying too much such finer nerves and vessels."[50] In its attention to such parts, *An Essay on Man* reviews what Robert Morris would call the "whole," rather than the "fractions."

According to *An Essay on Man*, interest and self-love are related, and more importantly, they differ from disinterestedness and reason; disinterestedness is more reasonable than interest or self-love. Where reason sees the vista, self-love "sees immediate good present sense; Reason, the future and the consequence" (2.73–74). But by focusing on the near, the close, and the "immediate," self-love is reminiscent of the Palladian fractions (or political factions). Again in spatial terms, *An Essay on Man* casts interest, or self-love, as "temptations" that "throng," this word being associated with a crowd, or a mob, and the city. Murray Krieger suggests that "one need not press this spatial language, or its metaphysical construct, very hard before sensing its sociopolitical implications."[51] Indeed, Pope's use of spatial metaphors—"at distance and in prospect"—replays political assumptions that are already implicit in the neo-Palladian idea of the villa. Because it focuses, literally, on the whole, which it sees in prospect, reason is like a villa: both afford the owner a view of the whole, a prospect unobstructed by "throngs." So, according to *An Essay on Man*, self-love is to reason as the city is to the villa; self-love crowds in on moderate reason's attempts to maintain a prospect from which it can continue to survey the whole.

While on one level the argument of the poem makes these points, the structure of the poem on another level complements the spatial distinction. As is well known, the beginning and end of almost every line in the *Essay on Man* contain a rhetorical extreme, an antithesis. Martin Kallich tabulated this technique and concluded that "the figure of antithesis appears . . . three hundred [times] in 1285 lines."[52] For example, the last lines of the first epistle feature a series of these rhetorical antitheses:

All Nature is but Art, unknown to thee;

All Chance, Direction, which thou canst not see.

All partial Evil, universal Good. (2.289–94)

The antitheses lie in, among other things, the differences between Nature and Art, the narrator and "thee," partiality and universality, and Evil and Goodness. It seems that only those people who can afford to do so can reconcile such oppositions, that their reconciling requires a certain position, similar to that vista enjoyed by reason.

However, for Pope, and for the Palladians (or for an epic of disinterestedness), these seeming oppositions are already reconciled by their symmetrical arrangement. That is, it is more important to recognize that the antithesis only occurs on the level of meaning, when considering the content of the lines. Antithesis arises only from the difference between the meanings of the two ends. Considered more formally, the same antithesis is also a symmetry; each end of the line is the same structurally. (All antitheses are but symmetry, "unknown to thee.") Because a line has opposed meanings at its beginning and its end, the words are playing the same structural role, that of symmetrical opposition. What is usually thought of as the literary figure of antithesis thus allows Pope to implement the architectural, even Palladian, idea of symmetry. The systemic disposition of these antitheses thus constitutes a series of structural symmetries, a Palladian "reflective symmetry," in which "the shapes have to be mirror images of each other."[53]

With such tensions at the beginning and the end, the center cannot hold. Quoting *An Essay on Man*, it could be said that with rhetorical oppositions on either side of the caesura, each line of the *Essay on Man* is "created half to rise, half to fall" (2.15). The difficulty in trying to reconcile these oppositions requires this space. Pope's couplets require some breathing room, and they find it in the space represented by the caesura. In the preface to *Madness and Civilization*, Michel Foucault puts forward a similar understanding of the caesura: it "establishes the distance between reason and non-reason."[54] In *An Essay on Man*, the distance between the apparently irreconcilable, between reason and unreason, is the length of the caesura, the pause in the middle of each of its lines. For those "fools"—a word which invokes the problem of being unreasonable—who cannot believe that "whate'er is best administer'd is best" (3.304), each line has its caesura, a pause in which they can catch their breath, decide where they stand, and move on. Pope refers to what we call a caesura as a "Hiatus, or Gap between two words," thus pointing out that each line has an open "space," or "place," between the "bounds."[55] In other words, in the middle of the line, in the hiatus, the framing elements of the poem open the middle section of each line.

Tillotson, who believes that "Pope's syntax is always as compressed as possible," argues that "his meaning is left to grow at leisure out of its confined context."[56] If it is in the ending of each line that Pope tries to effect closure, it is in the middle that meanings multiply. And in the middle of almost every line we find the caesura, a space very different from the "one unit" ending. These spaces, arranged so consistently throughout the poem, represent silences in the reading. Pope claims that "all great sensations dwell in Silence,"[57] a claim which suggests that the greatest parts of the *Essay on Man* occur in its hiatuses, in its caesurae. One could not be any more disinterested than to believe that the greatest sensations are silent or should be responded to in silence. The assumption that any great sensation must be described, must be spoken, comes out of the kind of dependence which this poem has set out to avoid. In fact, insofar as the great sensations cannot be spoken about, they are, in a sense, repressed, with the caesura again representing the line that separates the reasonable from the unreasonable.

After William Warburton wrote *A Vindication of Mr. Pope's* Essay on Man (1735), Pope wrote to him: "You have made my system as clear as I ought to have done and could not."[58] In his *Vindication*, Warburton

argued that "the best system," which he believed *An Essay on Man* represented, "must needs be such . . . as has a perfect Coherence, and Subordination in all its Parts." In its emphasis on coherence, subordination, and
the provision of a place for a every part, Warburton's critique of *An Essay
on Man* reformulates the Palladian ideal. In its use of antitheses, of the
rhyming couplet and of the caesura-axis, Pope's *Essay on Man* achieves
that coherence and subordination. Distributed along a central axis,
across which seemingly opposed elements actually merely reflect each
other, Pope's *Essay on Man* represents the reasonable disinterest thought
to be implicit in the idea of the Palladian villa. Everything has its place in
An Essay on Man. According to Warburton, Pope has thus given the
poem "the utmost Grace of Uniformity."[59] Pope himself believed that
Warburton was right. And within fifteen years that uniformity was the
poem's, and Pope's, greatest critical liability.

4

"Approach and Read . . . the Stone": Toward An Archaeology of Gray's "Elegy"

☙ "WE EXPORT YEARLY OUR OWN treasures into foreign parts by the genteel and fashionable *tours of France and Italy*, and import ship-loads of books relating to their antiquities and history . . . while our own country lies like a neglected province." Thus does William Stukely indict the British Palladian preference for buildings consonant with Continental architectural theory, contending instead that it is the "nativ furniture" of the early British "here," in Britain, that "we are to explore, to strike out their latent meaning."[1] When most architects were emphasizing the importance of proportion, symmetry, and uniformity, the work of architectural antiquarians such as Stukely, Walter Charleton, and John Aubrey indicates a self-conscious change in England's relationship with its past (or, considered in terms of contemporaries who persisted in designing variations on classicism, with the Continent).[2] Significantly, archaeologists eventually claim that stone circles such as Stonehenge represent not a dilapidated remnant of fine Roman uniformity, as had been previously thought, but rather, as

Edmund Burke would formulate it, a "grandeur" whose "art hides itself
. . . [in] seeming rudeness."[3] After these investigations, a lack of uniformity—a "seeming rudeness"—actually increases Stonehenge's perceived
importance.

Consequently, a historiography of Stonehenge in the seventeenth
and eighteenth centuries reveals the gradual emergence of an aesthetic
which would eventually topple the neoclassical aspects of, say, Milton,
Vanbrugh, or Pope. For in rejecting Roman, classical, or Continental
uniformity, Stonehenge archaeology redefines the concepts of nature and
of nation. Stonehenge comes to be considered more natural than a Palladian building precisely because it is either unfinished or dilapidated.
Natural here means neither uniformity nor order but either the disorga-
nizing effects of the passage of time or an admirably unpolished quality
inherent in the English nation: its natives are naturally rough-hewn. On
one level, architects in the second half of the eighteenth century (and
poets in the 1740s) claim the second law of thermodynamics as revenge;
things fall apart, naturally. It is unnatural to persist in the effort to maintain them as orderly. But this new appreciation of disorderliness constitutes, on another level, a political argument, the new valence of which
can be seen clearly when contrasted with Milton, whose (architectural)
training emphasized order and proportion.

For Milton, in the seventeenth century, nature meant a numerical
order underlying the universe, which allowed *Paradise Lost*, and by implication Britain, to participate in the world as an equal with other countries. Britain was like other nations: the natural proportion allowed
similitude. As Joseph Rykwert writes in his description of numerical
principles behind some architectural design, it was thought that numerical "harmony . . . would reconcile political and religious divisions."[4] By
the 1740s, with the reevaluation of Stonehenge, however, Britain is seen
differently. If the British can claim Stonehenge as an original piece of
British architecture, and if it survived in any way approximating its orig-

inal design, then the British must admit that some element of British-ness, some element of that nation, is by definition disorderly.

By involving the reader in an archaeological activity—"Approach and read . . . the stone" (115–16)—Thomas Gray's "Elegy Written in a Country Churchyard" assimilates the recent developments in British archaeology.[5] Commemorating the "rude forefathers" (16) of a hamlet buried in a previously "neglected spot" (45), Gray's "Elegy" reflects changes in historical and aesthetic perception concomitant with an eval-uation of the British past newly appreciative of native traditions. This change, like evidence in archaeology, is not particularly visible; despite the many eighteenth-century publications about, and references to, the important (and varied) origins of Stonehenge, this discussion remains more or less underground, both in the eighteenth century and in the study of the eighteenth century. (Stuart Pigott, for example, describes this early Stonehenge archaeology as "a sterile little controversy in mid-century.")[6] Literary history often reads Gray's "Elegy" as a nascent version of romanticism, as an answer to the question of where and when British romanticism originated.[7] But it is more difficult to ascertain where that nascent, or "pre," romanticism began; the concept of preromanticism describes the origins of romanticism without addressing the origins of preromanticism itself. However, reading the "Elegy" in the light of the emerging Stonehenge archaeology indicates that the "Elegy," and the pre-romanticism it supposedly represents, participates in an eighteenth-cen-tury reappraisal of British architectural history.

Although I focus on Thomas Gray and the "Elegy" here, I am also interested in, and obliquely referring to, a series of other works from the 1740s, such as Mark Akenside's "Pleasures of the Imagination" or Joseph Warton's "Enthusiast," which place the narrator in almost explicitly anti-Palladian spaces. Architectural publications and poetry from the 1740s show that changes in aesthetic and historical perception occur gradually; as is clear with Gray's "Elegy," the transition to a preference for all things

British is by no means finished in the 1740s. Like the reinterpretation of ancient British architecture, the "Elegy"'s revisions layer British on top of Roman. Although this chapter is concerned with developing a way of noticing that change as it is emerging, it is important to remember that the hesitation that accompanies this change is as meaningful as the change itself.

Little attention was given to Stonehenge in the seventeenth century, and when it was, people had difficulty with its rude disorderliness. According to one seventeenth-century commentator, Stonehenge survived by virtue of its own "weight and worthlessness."[8] In 1654, when John Evelyn visited Stonehenge, he recorded that "the stone is so exceeding hard, that all my strength with a hammer could not break a fragment."[9] His unsentimental attitude represents a typical seventeenth- and at least early eighteenth-century response to the stone circles. Throughout the eighteenth century most stone circles were considered valuable not historically or symbolically but frequently only insofar as they were made of otherwise usable stone. The stones of Avebury, for instance, were quarried, i.e., heated by fire and then doused with water so as to crack them into blocks small enough for building the walls of nearby houses.

Although Samuel Pepys agrees that Stonehenge was "worth going this journey to see," four days later he adds that "it was prodigious to see how full the downes are of great stones; and all along the valleys . . . which makes me think the less of the wonder of Stonage."[10] Perhaps even more in Pepys's time than in our own, Stonehenge was by no means the only stone circle. (Today, some stone circles, such as "The Sanctuary" near Marlborough, and parts of others, such as Avebury, probably the largest stone circle, are visible only because of concrete markers indicating where the stones once were.) Nor, despite the fame of Avebury and Stonehenge, were stone circles confined to the southwestern corner of England; Thomas Gray, for example, in a diary reporting on his trips to the Lake Country (1769), wrote that he "saw a . . . circle of large stones 108 feet in diameter."[11]

As controversial as his assumptions and conclusions became, Inigo Jones's claim that Stonehenge was Roman suggests something important about the mechanism of seventeenth-century British cultural appreciation, and it may be that his ingenious argument had something to do with the eighteenth-century rise of interest in Stonehenge. By claiming that Stonehenge was classical, Jones initiated the seventeenth and eighteenth century's Stonehenge controversy, by making Stonehenge more important that it had previously seemed. Working on a commission from James I, who had visited Stonehenge in 1620 during a "royal progress," Inigo Jones assembled *The Most Notable Antiquity of Great Britain, Vulgarly called Stone-Heng, on Salisbury Plain, Restored*, published posthumously in 1655 by his student John Webb. In this work, Jones claims, for two related reasons, that "*Stone-heng* . .. was a work built by the Romans." To begin with, Jones decided that Stonehenge was a dilapidated ruin. Then in his drawings, that is, what architects call a "plan," he provided the parts of Stonehenge he thought were missing. On the basis of these plans he argued that Stonehenge represented a Roman temple. Moreover, the scale of the work, according to Jones, was beyond the capability of the British. Regardless of whether or not Stonehenge is Roman, the Britons were incapable of building it because as "a savage and barbarous people," they were "destitute of the Knowledge, even to clothe themselves, much less any Knowledge had they to erect stately Structures, or such remarkable Works as *Stone-heng*."[12]

Through a principle of aesthetic noncontradiction, Jones argues that "where *Art* is not," i.e., among those British savages, "nothing can be performed by *Art*." Because Jones sees "Art" in this monument, art of which the British either are or were incapable, it must then have been built by the Romans: where art is, then can something be performed by art. However, considering Stonehenge as it stands, most interesting is Jones's assumption that the builders of the monument had art; for by "*Art*," he specifies that he meant "*order*," "*symmetry*," and "*decorum*," of which these Britains "neither had . . . in them."[13]

This contention means that unlike many other viewers, Jones believed that Stonehenge is ordered, symmetrical, and proportioned: Stonehenge had "*Art.*" Jones came to this conclusion by comparing his own stylized rendering, his own plan, of an imagined complete, circular Stonehenge, with Palladio's plan of an ancient Roman theater in Barbaro's 1556 edition of Vitruvius (figs. 8, 9). Although the surviving columns and lintels of the interior wall suggest an ellipse, Jones disregarded the physical evidence, invented interior hexagonal "walls," and

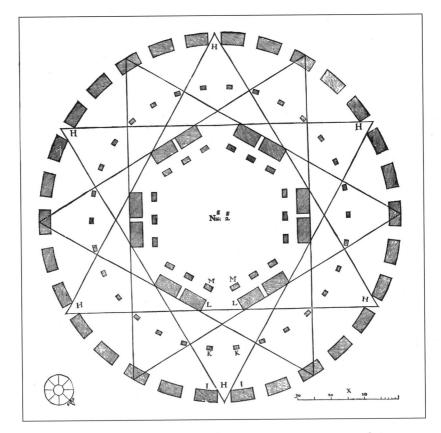

8. Plan of Stonehenge, Inigo Jones, *Stone-Heng Restored* (1655). (Courtesy of Avery Architectural and Fine Arts Library, Columbia University in the City of New York)

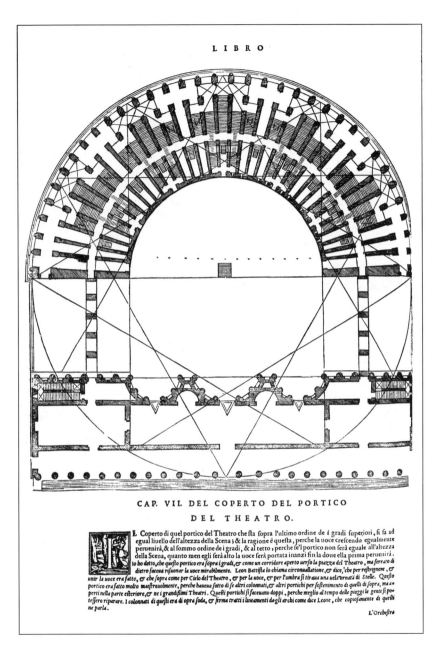

CAP. VII. DEL COPERTO DEL PORTICO DEL THEATRO.

E Coperto di quel portico del Theatro che sta sopra l'ultimo ordine de i gradi superiori, si fa ad egual liuello dell'altezza della Scena; & la ragione è questa, perche la uoce crescendo egualmente peruenirà, & al sommo ordine de i gradi, & al tetto, perche se'l portico non serà eguale all'altezza della Scena, quanto men egli serà alto la uoce serà portata inanzi fin la doue ella prima peruenirà. Io ho detto, che questo portico era sopra i gradi, & come un corridore aperto uerso la piazza del Theatro, ma serrato di dietro faceua risuonar la uoce mirabilmente. Leon Battista lo chiama circonuallatione, & dice, che per restrignere, & unir la uoce era fatto, & che sopra come per Cielo del Theatro, & per la uoce, & per l'ombra si tiraua una uel. tornatà di Stelle. Questo portico era fatto molto maestreuolmente, perche haueua sotto di se altri colonnati, & altri portici per sostenimento di quelli di sopra, ma da perti nella parte esteriore, & ne i grandissimi Theatri. Questi portichi si faceuano doppi, perche meglio al tempo delle pioggi le genti si po- tessero riparare. I colonnati di questi erà di opra soda, & firma tratti i lineamenti dagli archi come dice Leone, che copiosamente di questi ne parla.

L'Orchestra

9. Palladio, Roman theater, from Barbaro's edition of Vitruvius, 1556. (Courtesy of Avery Architectural and Fine Arts Library, Columbia University in the City of New York)

drew the outer wall of Stonehenge as a true circle. Jones then inscribed, within his Stonehenge plan, "four intersecting equilateral triangles corresponding to the ancient theater."[14] The ease with which these triangles fit inside Jones's version of the monument cinched his argument; the triangles showed that Stonehenge had "Art," that it had order and symmetry. And because the triangles fit into Jones's drawing just as they had in Palladio's, Jones concluded that the Romans built Stonehenge, just as they had supposedly built the theater that Palladio's illustration represents.

As Christopher Chippindale notes, "The best thing about the analysis is its nerve."[15] Inigo Jones drew his conclusions on the basis of highly stylized drawings of the monument as it might have stood, given his reading of its remnants, i.e., on inaccurate drawings. In fact, he drew his conclusions on the basis of a plan, which is like a map in that it represents spatial arrangements from above. His use of the plan points to its limitations as an analytic tool in architecture. As subsequent Stonehenge archaeologists saw, plans oversimplify. Plans must idealize, must stylize. They represent a scale version of topographical features only, seen from above. By definition, they are two-dimensional; the plan puts the viewer outside and above the object represented, looking down at a selected view of spatial arrangements. In a plan, one can only determine space laterally, from side to side; plans do not represent heights or surface textures.

Inigo Jones's argument, tying Stonehenge to the Romans, effectively initiated a series of responses, a Stonehenge controversy. For example, in *Chorea Gigantum: Or, The Most Famous Antiquity of Great Britain, vulgarly called Stonehenge, standing on Salisbury Plain, Restored to the Danes* (1663), Dr. Charleton, physician to Charles II, disagreed with Inigo Jones, telling the reader to "Behold, here, a notable Example of the *Discrepancy of Men's Judgments, even in Things easily determinable by the Sense!*" which might sum up the controversy considered as a whole. In any case, Charleton contends that he has "diligently compared" Stonehenge with monuments in

Denmark and argues that Stonehenge was "erected by the DANES. . . . and principally designed to be a Court Royal, or Place for the Election and Inauguration of their Kings."[16] Written so soon after Charles II's coronation, Charleton's suggestion gives a new meaning to the idea of Stonehenge "restored."

In a dedicatory poem, "To my Honour'd Friend *Dr. Charleton*, on his learned and useful Works; and more particularly this of Stone-heng, by him Restored to the true Founders," prefixed to *Chorea Gigantum*, Dryden alludes to the various histories associated with the monument:

> His *Refuge* then was for a *Temple* shown:
> But, *He* Restor'd, 'tis now become a *Throne*. (57–58)

The "His" and the "*He*" refer to the two members of the Stuart monarchies who visited Stonehenge. Like James I, but for reasons very different, Charles II, Charleton's patron, also spent time at Stonehenge: he hid there. In 1651, after the Royalist defeat at Worcester, a disguised Charles fled to England's south coast. While in hiding in Woodford, between Salisbury and Stonehenge, he and "his protector, Col. Robert Phillips . . . 'rid about the Downes, and tooke a view of the wonder of that country, Stoneheng.'"[17]

So Dryden's "His *Refuge*" refers to Charles II's 1651 visit to Stonehenge, while "a *Temple*" metonymically represents Jones's dismissed reading of the stone circle. And the chronology implied by "then" reminds us that Jones's reading of Stonehenge as a Roman temple was published only four years after Charles was in hiding around Stonehenge. Moreover, Dryden's use of an antithesis creates an undertone of irony: after the Restoration the same old stone temple has been surprisingly redefined as a throne. According to Richard Kroll, "Dryden's epistle constitutes . . a critical meditation on those motives by which a literate culture can differentiate among . . . older sources of authority."[18] It could be that it is Stonehenge itself which provides a vehicle for "critical meditation" on different older sources of authority. And for Dryden in the seventeenth century, the interpretations move from the temple to the throne, or in political terms, from the Civil War to the Restoration.

In 1665 John Webb, Jones's student and the publisher of his *Stone-Heng Restored*, defended Jones's Roman interpretation, contending that the Danish could not have built Stonehenge because after the fall of the Roman Empire, they, like Jones's British before the Roman Empire, were not capable of constructing such a building. According to Webb, the end of the Roman Empire was exacerbated by "the Rage of fierce and barbarous Nations" (such as Denmark, implicitly), and it was "attended with a general Confusion of all things throughout the Universe."[19] Not only was Stonehenge not built by the Danes, but in fact it fell into its present state of disrepair under their political leadership.

In the 1690s John Aubrey, Charles II's guide during his 1663 return to Stonehenge, permanently altered the Stonehenge debate by changing the method of research. Calling his method "comparative antiquity" and describing it as "a kind of algebraical method . . . to make the stones give evidence for themselves," Aubrey compiled and circulated in manuscript (but did not himself publish) the results of research he had undertaken on a commission from the duke of York. Aubrey considered the stone circles of Wiltshire in light of the other remaining circles spread unevenly throughout the British Isles, most of them in the north and west of England. He visited or had others collect evidence about such stone circles as Devil's Arrows (York), Arthur's Round Table (Cumbria), Caer Prewen (Wales), Boscawen-Un Stone Circle (Cornwall), and St. Buryon (Penzance).

Aubrey even found a stone circle in Ireland, at which point he remembers that "the Romans had no dominion in Ireland, or (at least not far) in Scotland: therefore those temples are not supposed to be built by

them: nor had the Danes dominion in Wales. . . . But all these monuments are of the same fashion, and antique rudeness; wherefore I con-
clude that they were works erected by the Britons."[20] By comparing the
stone circles with the known extent of Roman influence, Aubrey demonstrates that the circles were built by the native British, not the Romans.
His argument would forever change how the British look at the ancient
monuments that dot their landscape.

   It is difficult to overestimate the influence of this unpublished argument. When Daniel Defoe's *Tour* arrives at Stonehenge, for example, he
refers to the varied attributions put forward by Inigo Jones and John
Aubrey; clearly Defoe was familiar with this argument, circulated rather
than published. Moreover, Defoe calls Stonehenge "that celebrated piece
of antiquity, the wonderful Stone-heng." One hundred years earlier
Stonehenge had been described in terms of its "weight and worthlessness"; by the 1720s Defoe is calling it "a reverend piece of antiquity."[21] In
appreciating Stonehenge, Defoe positions himself as someone familiar
with several authors who had written on this relatively obscure subject.

   As important as were the consequences of Aubrey's discovery, even
more important was the method by which he came to his conclusion.
Unlike seventeenth-century historiography generally, and the Stonehenge controversy specifically, Aubrey did not proceed deductively on
the basis of established sources. Unlike Jones, he did not simply collate
all previous discussions of Britain or architecture from, say, Pliny, Caesar, or Camden, and then make his argument. Instead, he considered
both the historical, written records and the stone circle evidence, conjec-
turing that too many stone circles were outside the Roman sphere to
have been built by the Romans. That is, recognizing the limitations of
historical evidence, Aubrey used what we now call archaeological evidence.

   As a result of Aubrey's early archaeology, Stonehenge was no longer conceivably Roman, yet its importance grew, as Defoe's *Tour* suggests. "The elegant Roman and Danish Stonehenges were in decline, and the rude British was rising," writes Chippindale.[22] This change left eighteenth-century observers (and today's scholarship) with a problem: how could the importance of Stonehenge be accredited at the same time that England was going through a significant period of classicism? As Howard Weinbrot points out, "The danger or irrelevance of classical culture in a putative neoclassical age is not one of the more attractive paradoxes of literary history."[23]

Although Stonehenge was neither "worthless" nor Roman, the alternative that might make it even more worthwhile had not yet materialized. That is, if Stonehenge represented an archaeological remnant of an ancient Britain, then it must have been one part of a well-organized, now-forgotten British culture. The predicament that this archaeology consequently presented was how to describe the lost culture symbolized by the scale of Stonehenge. Enter the Druids. Able to assume that the stone circles were British, subsequent eighteenth-century archaeologists went on to demonstrate its connections to a Druidical culture. Although Aubrey suggests that stone circles "were Temples of the Druids,"[24] he actually distances himself from the idea, even changing the title of his manuscript from "Temple Druidum" to "Monumenta Britannica."

William Stukely, who eventually referred to himself as a Druid, did not share Aubrey's qualms, and in 1740 he published *Stonehenge: A Temple Restor'd to the British Druids*, in which his personal, psychological understanding of Stonehenge takes on an almost religious dimension: "A serious view of this magnificent wonder, is apt to put a thinking and judicious person into kind of ectacy." Unlike Jones's plan, Stukely's description of Stonehenge as he experiences it draws upon a theatrical vocabulary, with the viewer experiencing a catharsis-like involvement in the monument. According to Stukely, Stonehenge has "everything proper bold [and] astonishing"; it is "awful" and "august." In its emphasis on astonishment, this is the language of melancholy. It is also an aesthetic of sentiment; compared with, say, Pope, Stukely is more concerned with how a space would make one feel. Rather than describe the spatial relation between the parts in stylized, abstract terms, Stukely contends that "when you enter the building . . . you are struck into an exstatic *reverie*." Considered architecturally, his description and to some extent the illustrations in his book are more sympathetic to the view than they are to the plan.

In his description of what he imagines to be all viewers' responses to Stonehenge, Stukely remains self-conscious of the implicit theatrical, melodramatic, and sentimental tensions. In the actual stones—and "here," according to Stukely, "a single stone is a ruin"—Stukely sees an unresolved conflict between art and nature.[25] But in his description he overturns the general classical preferences: "The grandeur of that art [Stonehenge] hides itself. . . . For tho' the contrivance that put this massy frame together, must have been exquisite, yet the founders endeavor'd to hide it, by the seeming rudeness of the work."[26] Rather than disguising art in a natural proportion or symmetry, as, say, Jones might have done, for Stukely, Stonehenge intentionally hides its art under the natural rudeness of the work. Stukely sees the same rudeness that Jones and Webb dismissed; unlike them, he valorizes it. Although he also agrees with Jones that here "art is not," he goes on to claim that that artlessness proves that art is in fact there. Inverting Jones's principles, Stukely is claiming that where art is not, art is. The natural, here thought of in terms of the natural ruins of a lost culture, is preferable to art, art meaning whatever cultivated polish that would differ from "rudeness."

Even if Stukely rearranges Jones's priorities, however, even if the preferences have been reversed, he retains to a large extent Jones's terms: "art," "nature," "rudeness." In his *Choir Gaure* (1747), John Wood argues that "we may therefore turn the Tables, and instead of calling STONE-HENGE the BABEL of its BUILDERS, pronounce it the MONUMENT of their CRAFT."[27] Turning the tables describes what was happening in architectural titles from the 1740s. The natural represented by decay becomes preferable to the natural represented by order; the artfulness represented by rudeness becomes preferable to artfulness represented by a kind of polish. And the British have become preferable to the Romans. Turning the tables also describes what was happening in some of the poetry of the 1740s.

In a way, turning the tables is a tentative act; throughout, the terms, or what Wood describes as "the Tables," remain the same. Wood's hesitation to overturn the tables is important; it represents the relatively slow pace of change in the 1740s. For example, when Wood wants to show the greatness of ancient Britain, he argues that "King Bladud," the mythical founder of Bath, "traveled into *Greece*," where he studied under Pythagoras and "built . . . even the DELPHICK TEMPLE itself" (10), before returning to Britain to found the Druids. For Wood it was the (recently) important prehistoric British who taught the Greeks how to build the kind of architecture that we (mistakenly) call classical.

Despite his intention to make such a sizable claim on behalf of the ancient British, Wood begins with a quote from Caesar as his authoritative source, not so much for what Caesar said as for who he was when he said it: "Caesar! even Julius Caesar the High Priest of *Jupiter* and of *Rome* herself, undeniably proves the BRITANNICK ISLAND to have been enriched" (3). By appealing to Caesar's authority, Wood simultaneously demonstrates the importance of that Britannic island and relies on the acknowledged greatness of its Roman colonizers. Yes, Wood has turned the table, but it is the same table.

The 1740s' ambivalence over the difference or the similarity between the British and the Roman also emerges in John Wood's most famous work, the development of Bath, itself also an overlay of Roman and British. As Simon Varey writes, "In Roman guise, Bath as Wood wanted it would re-create the mythical British history that he was sketching in the late 1730s and early 1740s." In the case of Bath's Royal Circus, the façades, seen from the street or in elevation, mimic the three different column types of the Colosseum, with a new architectural order on each level. However, when seen from above, or in a plan, the diameter of the Circus's outer circle "matches the circumference of the present chalk wall at Stonehenge."[28] And Wood placed the entrances for the three roads of the Circus in line with the placement of the entrances into Stonehenge as drawn by Inigo Jones (republished in 1725, two years before Wood arrived in Bath).

In the early 1740s this combination of Roman and British figures in Batty and Thomas Langley's *Ancient Architecture Restored and Improved* and *Gothick Architecture, improved by Rules and Proportions*. As even the titles indicate, the Langleys' new appreciation for preclassical British architecture was, again, cast in terms of the classical rules. In *Ancient Architecture* they admit that "these *Modes* of *Building* . . . are condemned by many, on a Supposition that their principal Parts have been put together *without Rules*."[29] They are probably right, given the classical definition of rules: Gothic architecture would require very different rules. For example, in the Langleys' *Gothick Architecture*, one plate represents the elevation of a Westminster Abbey column, and the Langleys contend that the column's "general Proportions" can be determined if one "divide[s] the entire Height of the Column into 180 equal parts."[30]

It was in this architectural context that Thomas Gray developed a historical or, more accurately, an archaeological sensitivity to architecture, of which, he argues, the Langleys' rule-bound ethos of improvement was incapable: "Mr. Kent . . . had not read the Gothick Classics with taste or attention. he introduced a mix'd Style, wch now goes by the name of *Battey Langley* Manner." Gray's opposing "taste or attention" to the Langleys' "mix'd Style" suggests both his familiarity with the architectural publications of his day and the outline of his own architectural and aesthetic preferences. Thomas Gray records visiting stone circles, writes an "Essay on Norman Architecture," and within two years of its discovery visits Herculaneum, all of which suggest that he had firsthand knowledge of eighteenth-century archaeology.

Gray's architectural and archaeological education could be said to have begun during his tour of the Continent, during which, in 1740, he experienced firsthand probably the most celebrated archaeological site of the century up to that point: Herculaneum. While in Naples with Horace Walpole, Gray visited an archaeological discovery of a most exciting kind for someone raised in the wake of English Palladianism— a Roman city frozen around A.D. 79 (lost and extraordinarily well preserved when buried by Vesuvius). In December 1738, while digging a well, workers uncovered "some Pieces of Marble." Realizing that they had found the buried city of Herculaneum, one of the original participants, Nicolo Venuti, "causing myself to be let down with a Rope about my Middle . . . went about into the Cavern . . . [and] perceived it to be the Seats on which the Spectators set to see the Plays."[31] By tunneling out from the theater, they were able to excavate several complete buildings by 1740. Unlike Pompeii, which suffered a rain of fiery and weighty ash and pumice, Herculaneum was slowly swamped by an influx of a lavalike volcanic flow. The differences in the two materials have important consequences for archaeologies of the two sites. On the one hand, because of lava's cooling process, Herculaneum lay under fifty to sixty feet of stone; Nicolo Venuti says that "the great Quantity of Earth that had been laid over it . . . together with the Houses and other sacred Edifices built thereon, prevented" digging as much as he would have liked. Consequently, as Theodor Krauss explains, eventually "Pompeii took precedence [because] there the terrain was more easily dug into."[32]

According to a recent study by Joseph Deiss, however, the "rising volcanic mix, in fact, performed the useful function of preserving many upper stories of Herculaneum houses, whereas at Pompeii the upper portions collapsed from weight of ash and stone."[33] Because of the lava flow, Herculaneum retains more complete buildings than Pompeii, and Herculaneum streets retain their original feeling. At Pompeii the ashes, by burning the wood roofs, effectively left in their wake a plan. At Herculaneum the lava preserved the buildings, affording more of a view of the buildings and their vertical relationships with the streets and each other.

Writing from the site, Gray reports on the revelation of intact architecture, from structures—"parts of an amphitheater, many houses . . . [and] the front of a Temple"—to interior decoration, such as "pieces of painting . . . finer than any thing of the kind before discovered." And in an important, frustrating, and tantalizing passage, Gray announces that "the wood and beams remain so perfect that you may see the grain" but reminds his reader that they are "burnt to a coal, and dropping into dust upon the least touch."[34] Gray could only have learned this by actually touching the wood, and in so doing he damaged Herculaneum. On another level, however, the wood at Herculaneum constitutes an important archaeological find. As Gray learned at Herculaneum—with the wood itself—archaeology reveals elements of the past obscured by the written, historical record. According to Deiss, "The testimony of Herculaneum has shown that the amount of wood used in ancient building was greater than formerly supposed."[35] This Italian archaeology therefore contradicts the eighteenth-century vision of classical architecture. Similarly, Nicolo Venuti, one of the first people to visit the site, points out that the paintings discovered at Herculaneum (and taken to local estates) "are done in a Variety of Colours, among which are the Green and the Blue, which some people imagined the Antients were not possessed of, grounding their Supposition on a Passage in Pliny."[36]

The image of Gray going into the earth to explore an actual preserved Roman city represents a fascinating way of understanding changes that occur in the 1740s in Britain. In the process of confronting a place of almost mythic importance for early eighteenth-century

Britain—a town from the real Augustan Age—Gray realizes that this Roman town at least had not been what people thought it was. As soon as Gray can touch the real material of ancient Rome, it crumbles in his hand. Such a discovery not only changes what people thought about classical Rome, but it also alters the record for future visitors. With that crumbling wood, ideas about classical Rome also crumble, even if only slightly: a metaphor for the 1740s' change in perception regarding the Roman past.

Upon returning to England, Gray's tour informed his participation in an archaeological reevaluation of older preclassical English architecture. Gray begins to articulate a kind of English exceptionalism, according to which the English have always been less delicate and less polished than the Continent. As Gray argues in a letter written soon after his return, "Our poetry . . . has a language peculiar to itself."[37] But the British are not merely peculiar. He also claims that they have a peculiar indelicacy: "We are a reasonable, but by no means a pleasurable People."[38] Gray's "Essay on Norman Architecture" explains the "solidity, heaviness, and rude simplicity" of Norman architecture by positing a nativist version of natural architecture: "The artizans employed in them were probably subjects and natives of the country . . . unaccustomed to any other style of building." By simultaneously conceding that "they [did] not rather imitate the beautiful remains of a better age," Gray is arguing that the buildings are not "beautiful" precisely because they were built by the British. But their inability to imitate beauty, which Gray might call their uniquely British inability, does not impugn the importance of the architecture. In fact, it raises it. "These huge structures claim not only the veneration due to their great antiquity, but . . . have really a rude kind of majesty."[39] Such native buildings are important precisely because of their age, and concomitantly because of their rudeness.

The terms by which Gray appreciates Norman architecture—solidity, heaviness, and rude simplicity—are familiar from the Stonehenge controversy. To some extent, after his tour Gray employs a method in British literary history which this chapter has so far discussed with reference to archaeology. In his "Observations on English Metre," Gray states that he "would not . . . insert words and syllables, unauthorized by the older manuscripts, to help out what seems . . . defective in the measure of our ancient writers."[40] The usual assumptions about the structure and ornamentation of Roman houses run counter to Gray's method. By "completing" the interior wall of Stonehenge, "unauthorized" by the monument as it stood, Inigo Jones contravened Gray's method; similarly, by trying to bring proportion to Gothic architecture, the Langleys are performing on architecture the same kind of operation that Gray cannot condone in literature. They bring to the architecture elements unauthorized by the actual older buildings. For Gray (unlike the Langleys), older British literary and architectural traditions probably cannot be reduced to the rules of proportion, and they certainly cannot not be improved by them. Gray prefers those monuments, literary and architectural, with their rudeness intact.

Gray argues that the English language "was naturally rough and barren." In short, the British are, like Stonehenge, rude. And Gray opposes this natural British roughness to what he considers a troubling polish and delicacy. In "Some Remarks on the Poems of John Lydgate," Gray writes, "I fear the quickness and delicate impatience of these polished times, in which we live, are but the forerunners of the decline of all those beautiful arts which depend on the imagination."[41] In this inversion of previous aesthetic preferences, Gray argues that delicacy and polish, standard models of artistic success, actually presage a cultural decline. According to John Sitter, "All of the symptoms of sleepiness that Pope attributed ironically to the dunces and to Dulness . . . began to appear quickly in the 1740s as positive poetic values."[42] Gray prefers a lack of polish and goes so far as to argue that "regularit[y]. . . . of itself it hardly pleases at all."[43] In his "Observations on English Metre," Gray argues that "uniformity . . . is just the reason why we no longer use it."[44] That is, rather than being what it was for Pope and Warburton—the ultimate criterion of aesthetic value—uniformity itself precludes the use of uniformity. This rejection of "regularity" and "uniformity" could be said to represent Gray's acceptance of the new understanding of aesthetics concomitant with the reevaluation of ancient British architecture.

Like Stonehenge, a small parish Gothic church, or in Gray's essays the irregular writings of Chaucer, the British have always been rough and should claim that roughness as their own; here history, seen literally in the country's remains, both literary and architectural, becomes destiny. According to Joseph Rykwert, "The concept of 'national' slowly came to mean 'other than classical.'" In mid-eighteenth-century England, there were a few possibilities for that other-than-classical alternative, represented in architecture most dramatically by Stonehenge and to a lesser degree by the remaining preclassical, or Gothic, buildings. The eighteenth-century rise of "national architects" traced by Rykwert emphasizes "the native-born, the spontaneous, the natural, as against the foreign, the imported, the strange."[45] In England, as was not necessarily the case in Continental countries, the native was strange; in England, stone circles dotted the countryside. Architectural theory and Gray's literary theory accommodate that strangeness by making it naturally British.

The beginning of Gray's "Ode on a Distant Prospect of Eton College"—"Ye antique spires, ye antique towers" (1)—is as much an invocation of a nonclassical British past as it is about Eton College. Those "antique spires" predate the classical influences of the Continent; they, the narrator knows, are rough. And when the narrator describes how "once my careless childhood stray'd" (13), that "careless childhood" represents Britain's as much as it does any individual person's, in the same way that these individual "antique spires" represent ancient Britain generally. Just like Gray's use of the first person in his *Correspondence* to describe English literature—"our poetry"—the narrator's "careless childhood" spent among prickly Gothicisms stands for Gray's understanding of Britain's past. "We" grew up among "antique towers"; it is where "we" came from, it is where "we" will, like the narrator, return.

Similarly, Gray's "Elegy" confuses, or brings together, the British present and the British past. In fact, it is difficult to discern whether the poem figures the present in terms of the past or vice versa. Although the poem begins in the present—the "parting day" (1)—it very quickly returns to the past—the owl's "ancient solitary reign" and the "neglected spot" of the churchyard. The poem's initial, present-tense actors and activities simultaneously connote those of the past: "the lowing herd" and "the plowman . . . plod[ding]" (2, 3). The "solemn stillness" can be found in the return to a particular, nostalgic, stylized vision of the past, represented in part by the "plowman."

The transition from the figures of the present to those of the past, the movement from the wide-angle view across "the lea" to the close-up within the "Church-yard," is achieved by the owl that, in the third stanza, tears the placidity of the scene; with the entrance of the owl's cry, the verbs shift from "parting," "plodding," and "fading" to "mopeing," "complaining," and "molesting." And the owl, the figure on which this transition rests, is to be found in an "ivy-mantled tow'r" (9). The transition from the idealized scene of ageless agrarian stability is made by virtue of the exception that the tower represents: "save that from yonder ivy-mantled tow'r."

In a sense, the purported tranquillity of the British countryside is punctuated by these towers, these rough buildings. As Cleanth Brooks puts it, "The churchyard is described for the most part, not directly, but by contrast with its opposite: the great abbey church."[46] And because of Bentley's engravings for the poem, evidence exists as to what type of church buildings readers should imagine here. In the 1753 edition of

Gray's poems the "Elegy" was printed with four different engravings by
Richard Bentley, including a frontispiece (fig. 10), a headpiece, and an ini-
tial-letter piece (fig. 11), each of which was described in an appendix written by Horace Walpole and titled the "Explanations of the Prints." (In

10. Frontispiece, Gray's "Elegy," *Designs by Mr. R. Bentley for Six Poems by Mr. T. Gray*
(1753). (Courtesy of Rare Book and Manuscript Library, Columbia University in the
City of New York)

the case of one poem, "A Long Story," it was Thomas Gray himself who provided the original drawing, of a mansion, on which Bentley based his design for the engraving.) Referring to the frontispiece, Walpole describes "a Gothic gateway in ruins. . . . Thro' the arch appears a church-

ELEGY

WRITTEN IN A

COUNTRY CHURCH YARD.

H E Curfew tolls the knell of parting day,
The lowing herd wind flowly o'er the lea,
The plowman homeward plods his weary way,
And leaves the world to darknefs and to me.
                                                    Now

11. Title page, Gray's "Elegy," *Designs by Mr. R. Bentley for Six Poems by Mr. T. Gray* (1753). (Courtesy Rare Book and Manuscript Library, Columbia University in the City of New York)

yard and village church built out of the remains of an abbey. A Country man showing an epitaph to a passenger." This frontispiece literally acts as a gate to the poem, with the action of the poem occurring on the other side of the gate; on the other side of the frontispiece, someone whom recent scholarship calls "the Stonecutter" is showing the poem's epitaph to someone in the narrator's, or the reader's, position.

In the case, literally, of the initial letter, Bentley set a ruined Gothic church behind a capital T in Roman typeface, and as Walpole puts it, we have "an owl disturbed and flying from a ruinous tower." In reading the poem as it was published, then, we must first view a Gothic church. The owl that alters the focus of the scene is leaving a particular artifact of the British countryside. The visual text specifies the nature of the building. Concerned that reprinting these poems would upset many readers, Gray "desire[d] it may be understood . . . that the Verses are only subordinate, & explanatory to the Drawings, & suffer'd by me to come out only for that reason."[47] Hence, Gray prefers that readers see his poem as illustrating the visual text; he prefers that we see that "ivy-mantled tow'r" as a Gothic, preclassical remain.

As the narrator's focus narrows and sharpens, scanning down from the tower to "beneath those rugged elms" (13), the poem begins to consider people whom the narrator describes, significantly enough, as "the rude Forefathers of the hamlet" (16). To the extent that the "hamlet" represents rural, idyllic Britain, the "Forefathers" are then "our" forefathers, to use Gray's first-person pronoun. And to the extent that the "Forefathers" are the British forefathers, then the British are "rude." "Rude" is, "we" now see, what "we" have always been. The evidence of our hamlets shows us it is so.

These British are "frail," "uncouth," and "shapeless" (78–79), just like their ruined monuments, from the tombstones in the "Elegy" to the stone circles throughout the countryside (and both "neglected spot[s]" [45],

Stonehenge and the country churchyard, were burial grounds). The "Elegy" remembers not only the dead buried there, but their stone memorials as well; in the end, the poem serves as a prologue to an epitaph "graved on the stone" (116). In this sense at least, then, the poem can be said to invoke a figure like what Frank Ellis calls the "Stonecutter," someone "on whom the village would have to rely to frame" the memorial.[48] Regardless of whether that person is being addressed (as "thee") or described (as "him"), the "Elegy," in its epitaph, records the work of a stonecutter who preceded the poet in memorializing the dead in this country churchyard.

Whether directly addressed or not, the implied stonecutter represents the "Elegy"'s post-Stonehenge equivalent of what Gray elsewhere describes as a bard; in the wake of what we have seen as a critical reevaluation of Stonehenge, the stonecutter is to the builder what the bard is to the poet. Authentic, raw, truly British, in the terms of the Stonehenge debate. The stonecutter, providing the reader with the epitaph, insofar as it inscribed on a tombstone, becomes a figure for a new vision of the poet, or more specifically, an old vision of the poet: "th' unletter'd."[49] In this sense, then, from the past, or "from the tomb," does "the Voice of Nature" (91) cry. The native bardic tradition, buried in neglected spots, found in Britain naturally, comes alive in a reading of the stones that litter the British countryside. "Our" poetry is written on our ancient stones.

Here the voice of nature is actually the voice of the natives. The voice of the bard, or the work of the stonecutter, is natural because of its long-standing relationship with the British land. The significance of this redefinition of nature appears in a particular difference between the final edition of the "Elegy" quoted so far and an initial version, known as the Eton manuscript. In several important variations between the manuscript and the published version, Gray makes revisions that replay the overlay that characterized the debates about the origins of Stonehenge. Where in the final version of the "Elegy," the narrator refers to a "village-Hampden," a "mute inglorious Milton," and a "Cromwell" (57, 59, 60), the original refers to a "Village Cato," a "mute inglorious Tully," and a "Caesar."

Just as in the shift from considering Stonehenge Roman to some version of British, Gray's poem originally referred to Roman heroes but shifted to British ones. "We can be relatively certain," writes John Guillory, "that the prospect of a 'mute, inglorious Milton' focuses the largest and most intense anxiety in the poem."[50] The lost native British tradition is now considered important enough to lament by name, more important even than that of the classics. Moreover, in context, the British figures are used metonymically as a measure of comparison; the British authors now form a standard, one that Gray adopted rather than that of the Romans.

At the same time, it is equally important that Gray wrote both versions; because his initial impulse was for the classical references, the poem demonstrates not only a new and different national self-confidence but also a trepidation, or what Guillory refers to as "tension"; Gray did not immediately prefer the British model over the classical one. Only upon reflection did he choose the British. In other words, the fact that this important change came in the form of a revision tells us something about the 1740s. As Loftus Jestin points out, this tension between preferences inflects the very materials of the printed poem itself. According to Jestin, Walpole and Bentley's "decision to use Roman type everywhere . . . is further evidence of their neoclassical orientation."[51] They could have used, for example, a Gothic typeface.

Considering Gray's revisions, or more importantly, the seeming trepidation of his revisions, in the light of the Stonehenge controversy, the "Elegy" then does not simply come before a romantic tradition but at the end of a contested reconsideration of a native tradition. In fact, the "Elegy" recapitulates many aspects of the Stonehenge controversy. By the mid–eighteenth century Stukely and Burke prefer the view of Stonehenge over its plan, just as Gray's "Elegy" places a viewer-narrator alone in the landscape. Like the Stonehenge controversy, the "Elegy" valorizes the stonecutter and, like the controversy again, only slowly revises the perception of the countryside as British rather than Roman. Like the archaeology that facilitated the reconsideration of British architecture, Gray's "Elegy" figures British history in terms of layers, from the burial sites in the churchyard to the superimposition of British upon Roman in Gray's revisions.

5

"To Invent in Art and Folly": Walpole's *Castle of Otranto*

ꝰ UNTIL THE MIDDLE OF THE EIGH-
teenth century, proportion had provided a measure of the good and, according to some architects, an approximation of the divine; Horace Walpole's work commemorates the end of that possibility. Unlike Milton, Pope, and even Vanbrugh (whose varying from the rules occurred nonetheless within arguments over proportion), for Walpole the belief "that the Great Author of all things had . . . standards of . . . harmony, and proportion in his mind" represents "a kind of confession of being vanquished." The possibility of divinely ordered proportion represents an abandonment of belief, rather than its expression and confirmation, as it had been for Milton and Pope. Walpole describes his own invocation of the "Great Author" to justify proportion as "deserting argument." With Walpole, the possibility of (a divine) proportion, the very thing that had guaranteed the potentially universal symbolic viability of structure just 100 years before, has become a matter of (personal) belief. It cannot be proven in words—Walpole "might not probably be able to prove by

words the reality of *proportion*"—or, by extension, through argument.[1] Whatever had once animated the arguments over proportion is gone. The question for Walpole, as architect and as author, is what will replace it.

In a letter to John Chute, who helped redesign Walpole's Strawberry Hill, Walpole writes:

> I have not half the satisfaction in going into churches and convents that I used to have. The consciousness that the vision is dispelled, the want of fervour so obvious in the religious, the solitude that one knows proceeds from contempt, not from contemplation, make those places appear like abandoned theaters destined to destruction. The monks trot about as if they had not long to stay there; and what used to be holy gloom is now but dirt and darkness. There is no more deception. . . . One is sorry to think that an empire of common sense would not be very picturesque; for, as there is nothing but taste that can compensate for the imagination of madness.[2]

Visits to "churches and convents" make Walpole realize that there is nothing left for most people to believe; as he laments, we are left with "an empire of common sense." He longs for the time when "vision" entailed deception, if only because even that deception meant belief. Maybe such a belief was madness, but nowadays, says Walpole, where deceived "imagination" once was, we are left only with "taste."

According to Walpole, not only do arguments over proportion reduce the quality of a building to the mathematical relationship between its parts, they more importantly overlook the fact that most people do not exist in or experience a mathematical relationship with a building: "We do not admire a column because its shaft and base are sufficient to support the entablature: on the contrary all three are parts of *one* support." Walpole prefers to focus on the viewer's psychological response to a building. "One only wants passion to feel Gothic," according to Walpole's *Anecdotes of Painting*, where he adds that "Gothic churches infuse superstition—Grecian admiration."[3] Most people, according to Walpole, are more concerned about the look of a building, rather than how its proportions play themselves out across its parts. "Does one man in ten thousand on seeing an edifice consider whether the walls are of a proper strength and height?"[4]

Working in the wake of the reevaluation of British architectural history and its new appreciation for relatively disproportionate British architecture, Walpole draws upon what John Archer calls the "associational" techniques with which some architects were, in Walpole's terms, "imprinting the gloomth of abbeys and cathedrals on one's house."[5] According to Archer, associationalism represents an eighteenth-century British architectural innovation, "introduc[ing] a new manner of architectural composition" which "encouraged trains of associated thoughts in the imagination of the viewer."[6] Because the structure of a building, with the disposition of its parts made consonant through the bodily analogy (either in plan or in elevation), would have previously suggested the significance of its architecture, the associational type of composition becomes possible as the power of either classicism or proportion has waned. In the middle of the eighteenth century, British architecture begins to rely on the symbolic and historical associations in ornamentation, associations merely implicit in the actual building but potentially visible to the viewer. Robert Harbison describes this architectural impulse as "a way of seeing."[7]

Although Strawberry Hill and *The Castle of Otranto* are often considered as early instances of the Gothic Revival, Walpole would seem, as the source of a new style, more perspicacious than popular; the eventual popularity of so-called Gothic architecture or the Gothic novel was still at least twenty years away. However, rather than simply trying to revive a particular style for its own sake, Walpole uses Gothicism, or more accu-

rately, the signs of Gothic architecture, to investigate more or less theoretical issues regarding architectural proportion and association. Walpole is more interested in those issues than in Gothic architecture per se.
In this, Walpole agrees with Pugin's famous complaint concerning this
kind of architecture: "What could be more absurd than houses built in .
. . the castellated style? . . . Turrets so small that the most diminutive
sweep could not ascend them! The kitchens alone are real; every thing
else is a deception."[8] Walpole, however, aims to achieve that deceptive
absurdity: he enlists Gothicism for his interest in the degree to which
viewers' or readers' associations might be accepted as the truth—believing a new building to be authentically old, for example (and how that
susceptibility points out important perceptual problems). In a sense,
Walpole uses the Gothic as an example of issues implicit in emerging
architectural theories to criticize what Peter Sloterdijk has recently
called "the universally widespread way in which enlightened people see to
it that they are not taken for suckers."[9]

As *The Castle of Otranto* combines an argument over what might
replace proportion with the importance of vision, the possibility of
deception, and the potential madness of belief, it is interesting that Walpole should write approvingly of Chatterton's poetry, which was, like *The
Castle of Otranto*, initially framed as a discovery. While this chapter is not
centrally concerned with the literary forgeries of Chatterton or
MacPherson contemporary with Walpole's Strawberry Hill and *Castle of
Otranto*, Walpole's response to Chatterton nonetheless suggests the possibility of overarching connections between, and motivating impulses
behind, several artists working in the 1760s. Although Walpole made his
comments after the publication of *The Castle of Otranto*, the basis for his
admiration of Chatterton's forgeries is still significant. On the one hand,
Walpole is impressed by Chatterton's ability to fool the reader, considering it principally in relation to the audience's susceptibility: "When I consider what credulous oafs Chatterton found, I am less surprised at his

attempts."[10] On the other hand, however, Walpole applauds what he describes as Chatterton's ability to "invent both in art and folly," contending that "so versatile, so extensive, so commanding was [Chatterton's] genius, that he forged architecture and heraldry."[11] For Walpole, genius is found not in originality but instead in the ability to copy, and to copy so effectively as to convince people that new work is in fact someone else's ancient work. "I should be more proud of having imitated," writes Walpole in the second preface to *The Castle of Otranto*.[12]

Recently, Dianne S. Ames has argued that Walpole's Strawberry Hill "may be viewed *as* it would be *if* it were a Gothic castle."[13] In Walpole's terms, it imitated. What she calls an "as if" quality of Strawberry Hill—its "association" in Archer's terms—also obtains with *The Castle of Otranto*; it may be viewed, and indeed was initially viewed, "as if" it had really been "found in the library of an ancient catholic family in the north of England" (3). Although considering *The Castle of Otranto* in relation to Walpole's architecture has the advantage of rejoining what were for Walpole the already related activities of literature and architecture, more specifically it also suggests how contemporary architectural issues inform *The Castle of Otranto*.[14] In mid-eighteenth-century Britain he had available to him an architectural genre devoted to what Ames calls an architecture of the "as if": the folly.[15]

Usually in imitation of ruins, the British folly had "its heyday between 1730 and 1820." Although a few buildings had previously been designed to imitate the Gothic, "it was not until the English, striving to achieve an effect quickly and economically, started to use inferior materials, or simply went over the top . . . that these ornamental structures really began to deserve to be called follies."[16] Walpole, for example, contending that "the form is considered, not the materials," used "lath and plaster" to finish several rooms in Strawberry Hill.[17] Under these building conditions, mid-eighteenth-century Britain saw a boom in folly building. When considered in terms of Walpole's interest in the mid-eighteenth-century British fad for architectural forgeries, known as "follies," "sham ruins," or "Artificial Pieces of Ruin," Strawberry Hill and *The Castle of Otranto* constitute follies.[18] Like what Walpole calls the "false-Gothic" architecture of a folly he refers to as "the devil's cathedral," *The Castle of Otranto* self-consciously raises questions of proportion and authenticity, re-creating the past through contemporary associations concerning it, historical accuracy or a regular, proportional scale being less important than the inaccurate perception of historicity.

Midcentury follies include Horton Tower, also known as Sturt's Folly, built so that Humphrey Sturt could view the deer on his estate in Horton, Dorset; the ruinated Triumphal Arch at Castle Hill in Filleigh, Devonshire, built by William Kent (1730); the garden buildings at Stowe, especially Gibbs's Gothic Castle, which prompted Walpole to write "in the heretical corner of my heart I adore the Gothic building, which by some unusual inspiration Gibbs has made pure and beautiful and venerable" (1740–45);[19] the buildings at Painshill Park, Surrey, Charles Hamilton's garden, including the supposedly "Ruined Abbey" (figs. 12, 13); Grange Arch, Creech, Dorset (1746); Mow Cop, the supposed hilltop remains of an ancient castle, dominating the peak of an 1,100-foot mountain in Congleton, Cheshire (1750); Westerton Folly, a circular stone tower placed in the village green of Bishop Auckland, Durham (1750); Rodborough Fort, a sham castle built near Stroud, Gloucestershire (1750); Upcott Folly—a partially "destroyed" castle wall—near Barnstaple, Devonshire (c. 1760s); the Sham Castle, Wimpole Park (1768–72); Goldney's Tower, Bristol (fig. 14); and Blaise Castle, also in Bristol (1776).

A brief description of a few such follies illustrates how these buildings, as a genre, were designed, without regard to classical proportion, to fool the viewer. In 1760, at Auckland Castle in Durham, Bishop Trevor built a scale version of a castle with a cloister on the exterior to provide shelter for the deer population in the estate's park. At Arnos Castle, in

Bristol, William Reese used black copper slag to build stables designed in the shape of a castle, with castellated turrets and keeps (fig. 15). When Walpole saw it in 1776, he wrote about his surprise upon eventually recognizing that "it was an uniform castle, lately built, and serving for stables and offices to a smart false-Gothic house on the other side of the road."[20] With a folly, things are not what they seem, and that is one rea-

12. Ruined Abbey, front, Painshill Park, Surrey (1738–73)

son why people built them: e.g., Ralph Allen's Sham Castle, a freestanding wall arranged to imitate a ruined castle (fig. 16), or Horton Tower, a supposedly medieval tower built solely for watching the local deer population.

The fact that many of the early follies, such as those at Stowe or the Auckland Castle Deer House, were built in gardens has consigned them

13. Ruined Abbey, back, Painshill Park, Surrey (1738–73)

to a lesser role in architectural history; they are thought of as mere "out-buildings."[21] But in the eighteenth-century British context, these garden buildings instituted significant and lasting innovations. When Burke, for example, claims that "our gardens, if nothing else, declare, we begin to feel that mathematical ideas are not the true measures of beauty," he could mean both the vegetation and the buildings.[22] For these follies, even as garden buildings, hint at the possibility of designing seemingly

14. Goldney's Tower, Bristol (1737–64)

ill-proportioned buildings; they incorporate into the built environment the changes implicit in the rereading of Stonehenge and stone circles. The irregularity of these garden follies represents an alternative to the governing building styles. Like Burke, Walpole appreciates the new, irregular architecture emerging from these buildings:"I am as fond of the *Sharaggi*, or Chinese want of symmetry, in buildings, as in grounds or gardens."[23] The garden folly offers the possibility of a contemporary, irregu-

15. Arnos Castle, "The Devil's Cathedral," Bristol (c. 1740)

lar building style. For a Palladian like Robert Morris, this irregularity is the problem with follies; in his *Essay in Defense of Ancient Architecture* (1728), he inveighs against them as "base and contemptible Inventions . . . deform'd and irregular Compositions" (9).

As Burke understood, buildings such as a castellated stable or a monastic deer house showed the possibility of superseding the analogy between a building and a human body, an analogy developed by Vitruvius and reiterated in architectural texts into the eighteenth century. Vitruvius, for example, argues that from "the human body . . . comes the symmetric quality of eurhythmy; so is it [in] the completed building"; Alberti, referring to the "bones of a building," argues that when architects "considered man's body, they decided to make columns after its image"; and Wotton argues that "surely there can be no structure, more uniform, than our Bodies in the whole figuration: Each side, agreeing with the other, both in number . . . and in the measure of the parts."[24] Burke calls

16. Ralph Allen's Sham Castle, Bath (1762)

such formulations a "forced analogy" and sarcastically reminds us that "no two things can have less resemblance or analogy, than a man, and an house or temple; do we need to observe, that their purposes are entirely different?" Burke wonders why "artists . . . have not . . . accurate measurements of all sorts of beautiful animals to help them to proper proportions."[25] Although Burke offers this possibility only as a joke, such proportions had already affected the design of buildings, in the deer house, for example. The height of folly.

Allesandra Ponte distinguishes between "two opposing interpretations of the origins of architecture" in the eighteenth century: the first was the Vitruvian belief in the building's mimetic representation of the body; the second "focuses instead on the idea of [architecture's] symbolic origin."[26] Burke's *Enquiry* and, for example, the deer house, represent the second, symbolic school. According to Anthony Vidler, the type of late eighteenth-century "bodily projection in architecture" under examination with the follies was less physiological and more psychological. Rather than imitating the proportionate ratios supposedly evident in the stylized body, the psychological bodily projection saw the building "as objectifying the various *states* of the body, physical and mental."[27]

It is this mental and psychological "projection" to which Bernard Tschumi, whose own architectural practice today includes building (and theorizing) follies, alludes when he reminds us that a suggestion of madness occurs in the etymology of the word *folly* (not to mention the architectural history of the building type): "The word 'follies' was meant to be ironical, playing with the concepts of uselessness and excess generally associated with the built meaning, and with its other, primarily French definition meaning madness (*la folie*)."[28] Follies are both a kind of madness and a kind of building, a mad kind of building. For Tschumi, the folly holds out the possibility that "autonomous fragments can be recombined through a series of permutations whose rules have nothing to do with those of classification."[29] By undermining classifications such as the

historical (new or old?) or the functional (home or estate partition?), follies can seem mad. By disregarding a conventional sense of scale, by oper-
ating with an altered scale of proportion, follies have the effect of altering a viewer's perception.

Mid-eighteenth-century architects understood that this associative
architectural principle could lead to a variety of different responses to a
building. In *Familiar Architecture* (1768) Thomas Rawlins contends that by
viewing buildings, "the soul may then be said to be tun'd and exhilarated
by the Objects which strike the Attention." Here the psychology of the
viewer changes with the building under consideration, which implies a
new and important flexibility, not to say vacillation, in architectural criticism. As a consequence of this new primacy of viewer response, Rawlins distinguishes two opposed building types not structurally but rather
emotionally: when we see classical architecture, we are "awe-struck"; with
a "pleasing rural Cot" we are "sooth'd and mollify'd."[30]

Generally, however, the symbolism implied by the folly suggests the
building's supposed historical period; to most viewers, a sham ruin is
Gothic—despite the fact that practically all such ruins were built after
1740. Consider, for example, Joseph Heely's response to visiting a building designed by midcentury architect Sanderson Miller; despite the fact
that he knows the building either imitates or recollects the past, Heely
writes that he has "no doubt that an antiquarian . . . would sigh to know
in what aera it was founded, and by whom:—what sieges it has sustained;—what blood has been spilt upon its walls."[31] Heely knows that
it was founded in the present era by Sanderson Miller, that it has sustained only the sieges of visitors, and that, barring accidents in the course
of building, it has most likely avoided the spilling of blood. Yet he is
deluded into considering it historically.

Walpole responds to one of Sanderson Miller's buildings by writing
that "it has true rust of the Barons' Wars."[32] William Shenstone praises
Miller for "turning every bank and hillock of his estate if not into classi-

cal at least into historical ground."[33] But historical is precisely what a newly renovated and landscaped estate is not. To claim otherwise is almost madness, i.e., folly. But it is a folly that this building type induces in midcentury viewers. Benton Seeley describes the "Artificial Piece of Ruin" at Stowe by contending that "those who have but seldom seen [it] ... have their Memories refreshed at a Distance."[34] The paradox here— the central one in follies and sham ruins—is the fact that the viewer's memory is being "refreshed" by a relatively new object. The sham ruin represents, as Seeley's comments suggest, a contemporary vision of the past, rather than evidence from the past itself (which may be why the memory is most easily refreshed at a distance). As one eighteenth-century architecture critic, John Gwynn, complained, "Many of [Gothic architecture's] old inventions have been copied under the name of new discoveries";[35] these "new discoveries" are merely new, and not discoveries.

With Strawberry Hill, which he occupied in 1747 and purchased in 1748, Walpole replays the follies' historicism and their altered scale. His descriptions of the house indicate that he is participating in an argument over architectural proportion: "I am going to build a little Gothic castle at Strawberry Hill. If you can pick me up any fragments of old painted glass, arms, or anything, I shall be excessively obliged to you."[36] His remodeling of Strawberry Hill will result in "a little" castle, and perhaps in part because of its scale, it requires "fragments"—small parts of the past—to make it seem authentic. Later, after beginning to remodel Strawberry Hill, Walpole writes: "As my castle is so diminutive, I give myself a Burlington-air, and say, that as Chiswick is a model of Grecian architecture, Strawberry Hill is to be so of Gothic."[37] Again Walpole describes himself as building a "diminutive" or "little" castle. But here the fact that it is small only makes it more important; Strawberry Hill becomes a "model," both a scale copy of a larger original and also a pattern or example for emulation (fig. 17). Eventually, Strawberry Hill became a model house in another sense—attracting tourists who "initially had to produce a written note, then from 1774 a signed and dated printed ticket, and by 1784 a printed page of rules annotated at the bottom with the name, date of visit and number of visitors to be admitted."[38]

Of course, this altered scale is one of the most prominent features of Strawberry Hill, particularly in its interior. The bookcases in the library, for example, are "compressions of the choir screen at Old St. Paul's";[39] similarly, "in the north bed-chamber, when he wanted a model for his chimney-piece, he thought he could not do better than adopt the form of Bishop Dudley's tomb in Westminster Abbey."[40] When he invites Thomas Warton to visit Strawberry Hill, Walpole tells him that "some miniatures of scenes of which I am pleased to find you love—cloisters, screens, round towers, and a printing house, all indeed of baby dimensions, would put you a little in mind of the age of Caxton."[41] According to Walpole, these "miniatures" of "baby dimensions" will remind Warton of the architecture he had studied and chronicled. But Walpole does not

17. Strawberry Hill (1748 on)

say "remind"; he says "put you a little in mind of," almost as if he is suggesting that the scale of the Strawberry Hill buildings will affect Warton's perception.

By culminating in a scene which imitates the building of a ruin, *The Castle of Otranto* participates in the contemporary archaeological interest in nonclassical architecture generally and in mid-eighteenth-century British folly building specifically. Walpole's novel parodies classical architectural theory, especially its use of the stylized human body as the measure for establishing proportionate ratios. Architecturally, Walpole's parody investigates what "good" architecture might mean if proportion were no longer the governing criterion. In his other writings Walpole often emphasizes what he considers to be material connections between the novel and architecture, arguing that architecture—particularly that of his own "Gothic Castle," Strawberry Hill—prompted him to write *The Castle of Otranto*. According to his *Description of the Villa*, Strawberry Hill was "the scene that inspired the author of *The Castle of Otranto*."[42] More important, perhaps, is the fact that in describing how *The Castle of Otranto* would remind people of Strawberry Hill, Walpole should use the same phrase—"in mind of"—which he had previously used to describe how Strawberry Hill would remind visitors of "the age of Caxton." Walpole's claim that in *The Castle of Otranto* "you will even have found some traits to put you in mind of this place"—Strawberry Hill—not only invites comparisons between his literature and his architecture, it also involves the medievalizing altering of perception that characterizes the mid-eighteenth-century British folly.[43]

From the beginning of the novel, it is the possibility of the castle's existence that helps to generate the novel's deception (or realism). In the preface to the first edition, the supposed translator believes that "the scene is undoubtedly laid in some real castle" (5). The translator suggests that readers look for architectural details in the novel (and, by extension, imagine such a castle somewhere in Italy). The novel, at least, does not disappoint: there is "a subterraneous passage which led from the vaults of the castle to the church of saint Nicholas"; "the lower part of the castle was hollowed into several intricate cloisters"; there are "battlements in the tower above"; two characters sit in "the recess of the oriel window" (25, 38, 96). Like what Barthes calls a "realism effect," the inclusion of this relatively technical architectural vocabulary—"vaults," "cloisters," "battlements," and "oriel window"—increases the possibility of the castle's existence. With the castle's architectural details serving as important elements in the attempt to perpetrate a forgery, the first, forged preface concludes with a consideration of this supposed castle, launching the reader into the book with an architectural discussion.

According to the preface to the first edition, the story, "found in the library of an ancient catholic family in the north of England," was printed in 1529, took place during the Crusades, and was set "in some real castle" (3, 5). If this preface is to be believed, if a castle of Otranto did exist, then there should be a ruin in southern Italy where it once stood (an idea very attractive given the burgeoning interest in archaeology). But because the castle did not exist, by seeming to create its ruins, Walpole has in a sense built a mid-eighteenth-century British sham ruin—pretending to suggest historical period through detailing and a state of disrepair. With a folly, historicity is more important than historical accuracy; in the novel, the fact that people believed that the castle might have existed is more important than the fact that it did not. It is this belief in the castle's possible existence that makes both it and the novel a kind of folly.

During the same year he published the novel, Walpole wrote to Sir Horace Mann, describing his response to a French visitor who believes that Strawberry Hill lacks *la solidité anglaise*. Walpole complains that "the moment it is settled at Paris that the English are solid, every Englishmen must be wise, and if he has a good understanding, he must not be allowed to play the fool!" To play the fool is to engage in folly, precisely what Walpole does in Strawberry Hill and in *The Castle of Otranto*. Walpole goes on to explain that he "like[s] both sense and nonsense, and the latter better than what generally passes for the former."[44] (Like an architectural folly, not only does *The Castle of Otranto* suggest that he prefers nonsense to sense, it also demonstrates the difficulty in distinguishing between the two.)

Like Heely and Shenstone responding to Sanderson Miller's supposedly historical architectural follies, some early readers were duped into believing that Walpole's supposedly found novel, *The Castle of Otranto*, might be authentically medieval. William Mason, for example, wrote that "when a friend of mine . . . returned it [to] me with some doubts of its originality, I laughed him to scorn."[45] Articles in *Critical Review* (January and June 1765) and in the *Monthly Review* (February and May 1765) both tentatively accepted the novel's premise, until, with the second edition, "that indulgence we afforded to the foibles of a supposed antiquity, we can by no means extend to the singularity of a false taste in a cultivated period of learning," as John Langhorne laments in the *Monthly Review*.[46]

The translator who purportedly wrote the preface to the first edition warns readers that "belief in every kind of prodigy was so established in those dark ages, that an author would not be faithful to the *manners* of the times who should omit all mention of them. He is not bound to believe them himself, but he must represent his actors as believing them" (4). But by admitting in the second preface that he himself had written *The Castle of Otranto*, Walpole demonstrates that belief in at least certain kinds of prodigy is still alive in eighteenth-century England. Like Manfred's ability to see his daughter in a darkened chapel, the readers' ability to determine the truth is compromised by their susceptibility to the vagaries of perception. The first preface warns that "such a work . . . would enslave a hundred vulgar minds" (3); as it turns out, of course, the "enslaved" minds are those of readers who fall for the illusion—Walpole's enlightened audience.

In the second preface, as Walpole admits to having been the author of *The Castle*, he apologizes to "his readers for having offered his work to them under the borrowed personage of a translator" and begins to explain his reasons for having written the novel (7). Although he makes a series of binary arguments about England and France, the natural and the rule-bound, the ancient and the modern, for this chapter it is most significant that he should claim a preference for the oration of Brutus on the grounds that it is "affectedly unaffected" (9).

The phrase "affectedly unaffected" deserves some attention, for like a folly, Walpole's *Castle of Otranto* relies on affect; both work only if people believe in them or respond emotionally to them. Walpole's novel works best if people are "affected" enough to believe, for example, that Italy had Gothic architecture. Like a successful folly, the novel also must not suggest too overtly the possibility of forgery; it must, in other words, seem "unaffected" or natural (which, in the case of a sham ruin, means historical). But as soon as a contemporary production, such as an architectural folly, Strawberry Hill, or *The Castle of Otranto*, must seem natural, then it is, ipso facto, "affected," in the sense of artificial or pretending. It must seem to be what it is not. A folly, like *The Castle of Otranto*, is what it is not; it is historical, and it is not. It is, in the preface's terms, "affectedly unaffected." *The Castle of Otranto* exists in a tension between affected and unaffected.

Like a folly, the novel, having raised the possibility that its supposed castle might actually exist, tells a story in which, from its surprising beginning to its ambiguous ending, readers are left wondering whether anything is what it seems. When the novel begins, Manfred is attempting to marry his son Conrad to Isabella. When Conrad dies, Manfred blames a young peasant, Theodore, and then tries to divorce Hippolita, his wife, so as to marry his dead son's fiancée, who has fled the castle.

After the parish priest, Father Jerome, claims Theodore as his own son, a knight, Frederick, arrives at the castle, claiming to be its rightful owner. Is Theodore a peasant? Has Father Jerome broken his vows? Is Manfred not the castle's owner? Who is Frederick? Does he own the castle?

After a giant ghost, or the ghost of a giant, rises out of the castle, destroying part of it, and, while ascending to heaven, declares that Theodore is the rightful heir, these questions regarding identity and authenticity begin to be answered (although the violent ascension of a giant ghost raises a host of other questions). Manfred admits that his ancestor had poisoned Theodore's grandfather Alfonso and that "a fictitious will declared [Manfred's grandfather] his heir" (109). Manfred admits, in other words, that his residence in the castle of Otranto rested on people accepting a forged document as authentic. Father Jerome then explains that before joining the priesthood he had married Victoria and Alfonso's daughter, with whom he had Theodore. Jerome offers to prove his case by claiming to "have an authentic writing" (110). Although Manfred counters that he "needs [it] not," one cannot help but wonder whether Manfred has learned his lesson and puts no more faith in documents, or if he has not learned and therefore invests too much in what he calls "the vision we have but now seen" (110). In the end, the novel is still comparing vision and writing and forcing the reader to decide which one, if either, is more likely to provide the truth.

It is particularly difficult to decide whether vision is preferable to documents at the end of the novel, if only because throughout it, characters, Manfred in particular, undergo disturbingly rapid changes of perception. Soon after discovering his son dead, Manfred, walking "with disordered steps," opens his door to his daughter Matilda, "and as it was now twilight, concurring with the disorder of his mind . . . did not distinguish the person, but asked angrily who it was" (21). Later, in the castle's chapel, "guided by an imperfect gleam of moonshine," he stabs Matilda, whom he thought to be Isabella. After the attack, "Manfred, waking as from a trance, beat his breast, twisted his hands in his locks" (104). In both cases the partial lighting indicates the state of Manfred's mind, both its emotional state and its cognitive ability ("dark" and "disturbed").

Manfred's disordered mind reaches its frenzied peak when he mistakes Theodore for his thus-far-unacknowledged ancestor (whose line Manfred's family nearly ended by poisoning). Encountering Manfred and Theodore, Hippolita asks Manfred: "Why do your eye-balls fix thus?—What! cried Manfred breathless—dost thou see nothing; Hippolita? Is this ghastly phantom sent to me alone—to me, who did not— . . . . My lord, said Hippolita . . . command your reason. . . . What, is not that Alfonso? cried Manfred: dost thou not see him? Can it be my brain's delirium? . . . said Hippolita: this is Theodore. . . . Theodore! said Manfred mournfully" (80). Manfred cannot distinguish between Alfonso and Theodore, cannot distinguish the difference of generations, the different identities. He cannot distinguish between the original and the copy.

Perception is similarly limited in the case of the servants who discover what might be a giant living in the castle's great gallery. Diego, as "his hair stood on end," described "a giant," "for I saw a foot and part of his leg" (33). They concede that they have seen only part of the body, but from the fragmented vision they could extrapolate to a being of great size. The question for the novel's various characters then becomes whether to believe such an admittedly fragmented vision. The servants want the castle to be exorcised; otherwise they will refuse to continue working there. Hippolita, although she "no more than Manfred doubted of the reality of the vision," decided to assure . . . [Manfred] that the vision of the gigantic leg and foot was a fable" (35).

Not only do they see just a fragment, what they see forces them and the reader to begin to consider questions of proportion and scale. Framed and driven by the problem of proportion, the story told in Walpole's *Castle of Otranto* ironically dramatizes Walpole's sense that architecture designed principally on the basis of proportion is something more appropriate to the past. When the novel begins, Manfred has "contracted a marriage for his son" Conrad, because, according to "an ancient prophecy," "*the castle and lordship of Otranto should pass from the present family, whenever the real owner should be grown too large to inhabit it*" (15–16). Besides motivating the plot by seeming to provide an explanation for Manfred's interest in having Conrad married, this formulation specifically entails the problem of proportion: as the "real" owner gets bigger, the present inhabitants will become less likely to keep the castle.

The narrator rightly points out that "it was difficult to make any sense of the prophecy" (16). Besides proportion, it also raises the question of the authenticity of the castle's owner; should readers understand, at the very beginning of the story, that the castle is inhabited by people who do not belong in it? Considered another way, however, the prophecy would seem to imply not so much the difficulty of establishing the real owner but of determining whether the owner is in any sense real. Although a real owner could metaphorically grow too large for the building to contain him, either by taking him or herself too seriously or perhaps by acquiring too many possessions, no real owner could grow physically too large for a castle.

The narrative's initial prophecy entails all three implications: proportion, authenticity, and reality (and the novel enacts them in ways that replicate issues of contemporary architecture). For example, "an enormous helmet, an hundred times more large than any casque ever made for human being, and shaded with a proportionable quantity of black feathers," falls on—and kills—Conrad (17). This description raises questions regarding both proportion and the real. If a helmet 100 times too large for a human were to exist, it would actually have a disproportionate quantity of feathers (precisely the ironic possibility that the use of proportion in this extreme instance invites). Conrad is killed by a disproportionate helmet; the scale is wrong. And the helmet, in being covered with a "proportionable" number of feathers, is "grotesque," to borrow a word from the title of an architectural treatise by William Wrighte.[47]

The helmet, it turns out, belongs to a giant who has grown too large for the castle and is trapped in it, and who, at the end of the novel, destroys the castle as he rises: "A clap of thunder . . . shook the castle to its foundations. . . . The walls of the castle behind Manfred were thrown down" (108). This destruction gives a new meaning to the first prophecy's argument that the building will "pass" from its present owner. Although this verb might mean that ownership will be transferred, in this case the building itself moves, or passes. The giant's disproportion destroys the castle and simultaneously builds a ruin. In the end, then, Walpole's novel, which has relied throughout on questions regarding proportion and the authenticity, leaves a ruin—not only that of an individual building but of the idea of proportionate, orderly architecture which had governed British architectural theory for at least the preceding one hundred years.

Coda:
On Literary and
Architectural Form

இ DESPITE THE PERSISTENT BELIEF
that Palladianism was, as Giles Worsley has recently argued, "the domi-
nant approach to architecture in Britain from about 1615 to the last
decades of the eighteenth century," the one hundred years covered here
were characterized by remarkable stylistic diversity. Milton's proportion,
Vanbrugh's varying, Pope's uniformity, Gray's rude simplicity, and Walpole's Gothic forgery represent remarkably different approaches, especially for a period considered to be dominantly Palladian.[1] These changes
have important implications for both literature and architecture, implications that can inform each field. Because a connection between the two
fields can be found in their shared focus on form, literature can contribute to architecture as much as architecture can contribute to literature. For where literature uses *form* for meanings as different as narrative,
text, and structure, in architecture the word *form* has to do with shape,
and through that, with space. Like architecture, form is spatial. On the
one hand, architecture, as the shaping of space, offers a way of investigating formalism in literature; on the other, literature, in its focus on representation, offers important possibilities to architecture.

In *Sources of Architectural Form*, architect Mark Gelertner groups theories of architectural form into five synthetic statements and provides a
critique of each; by considering Gelertner's overview it can be seen how
literature can learn from and might contribute to architectural design
theory. Beginning with the idea that "an architectural form is shaped by
its intended function"—most famously formulated by Louis Sullivan in
the phrase "form is function"—Gelertner points out that many buildings
have a form that is more than is required by their function. According to
another theory of architectural design, "architectural form is generated
within the creative imagination," in other words, from an architectural
"genius," but Gelertner reminds us that there are nonetheless similarities
between buildings which make it difficult to cite them as isolated examples of such genius. It is also argued that "architectural form is determined by the prevailing social and economic conditions," but in contra-
diction to that theory, similar economic conditions can produce a variety
of different forms. As for the belief that "architectural form derives from
timeless principles of form that transcend particular designers, cultures,
and climates," Gelertner points out that few architects today would argue
that the Five Orders provide all the architectural knowledge a practicing
architect needs; he asks how this theory accounts for the invention of
new types and forms (e.g., the skyscraper).[2] It also seems that the variety
and change seen over the course of the period covered by this book, a
period of putative Palladianism, suggest that form does not necessarily
transcend designers.

Precisely for the degree to which it emphasizes the spatial quality of
architectural form, perhaps most intriguing is the idea that "architectural
form is shaped by the prevailing Spirit of the Age."[3] It would seem that
as the history of shaped spaces, architecture invites both spatial and stylistic consideration of form (Romanesque, the Gothic, the cruciform,
etc.). After all, it was architect Mies van der Rohe who claimed that
"architecture is the will of the age conceived in spatial terms."[4] In the

terms of seventeenth- and eighteenth-century classicism, proportion, as a mechanism for creating spaces with reference to shapes (a ratio of human height to the built height, or of the built height to built width, etc.), would then be one way of understanding architecture historically. However, Walpole's critique of proportionality points out that by the mid–eighteenth century in England, architecture no longer uses form—understood spatially—to resolve determinate historical conditions, that architecture is no longer the will of the age expressed in spatial terms per se. While the development of Strawberry Hill and the use of architecture in *The Castle of Otranto* indicate what architectural principles might replace proportion (and the difficulty of such a change), Walpole also tests the degree to which forms can be both spatial and historical; the fact that neither *The Castle of Otranto* nor Strawberry Hill is actually Gothic, i.e., medieval, reveals the limits of exclusively considering form spatially. Walpole's parodies recognize that form is no longer used spatially, thereby marking an important shift in the understanding of form and challenging whether it is still possible to understand form as historical. Those who would consider *The Castle of Otranto* or Strawberry Hill Gothic are wrong, precisely because of the forms; in other words, that which is called form created the impression (and that which is called form could disprove it).

Literature—the study of "*historical* products organized according to *rhetorical* criteria," according to Franco Moretti's definition—offers the possibility of imagining a way around this impasse in design theory: treat form as rhetoric.[5] Rhetoric fulfills many of the conditions set by design theory: it is generative, related to function and to social and economic conditions, and consequently to an age, without ever being a direct expression of any of them. Moreover, although there is a way in which rhetoric might be considered timeless, effective rhetoric, rhetoric in practice, must be timely, or in Kenneth Frampton's literary-architectural terms, "critical" and "contextual."[6] In the case of Walpole's Strawberry

Hill, for example, the seeming castellations, when considered in literary terms, constitute part of the rhetoric of the building; it is the rhetoric that leads to the supposed Gothic associations (fig. 18). Thinking that they are Gothic requires being persuaded into overlooking, for example, the "diminutive" scale. It requires overlooking, in architectural terms, form understood spatially. The "problem" that then haunts literary and architectural theory after Walpole is that people mistake rhetoric for form. At the same time, however, this misprision of rhetoric for form has the advantage of addressing the content vs. form conundrum. Walpole's

18. Strawberry Hill, detail (1748 on)

work suggests that form is rhetorical. That is why form can be apprehended as content (see Fredric Jameson or Hayden White); both form
and content are rhetorical.

Of course it would be inaccurate to say that all form is rhetorical.
Form is rhetorical only after it is no longer spatial, or after it becomes
stylistic. Or form is rhetorical only after Walpole, so to speak. In Walpole's architectural terms, form is rhetorical after proportion is no longer
the measure of a building's formal success. That is, in architecture, form
really is form (i.e., a spatial form) with, say, the Pantheon or the cathedral at Chartres. Similarly, in literature, form really is form (i.e., a spatial
form) in, say, terza rima. But Walpole's argument is that proportion, for
example, or that spatial understanding of form, is more appropriate to
the past. In the period covered by this book, it is Pope who could be said
to use form spatially—through the measured lines, the caesura, and the
rhyming couplet—for the last time; in fact, it could be precisely his spatial understanding of literary form that so bothered subsequent authors.
One could say that form understood spatially is a premodern concept,
and that the rhetorical understanding of form is modern (although it is
another question as to whether Pope is premodern, or whether he is
using literary form understood spatially to create the impression of a premodern, agricultural, villa lifestyle). Walpole's work, which is, in one
sense, formalistic but at the same time anachronistic or ahistorical,
marks this shift, either from the premodern to the modern or from the
spatial to the rhetorical understanding of form, a shift, in any case, which
had occurred before Walpole's proto-Gothic.

Generally, form is today understood in the way Walpole treated it—
as a kind of association, rather than as shape. Eighteenth-century
Gothic, for example, is thought to be theatrical, requiring and becoming
a stage set for a re-creation of the past (with Walpole an important figure, having hired set designers to build the interior of his Great Hall
with papier mâché). Giles Worsley, for instance, recently referred to

eighteenth-century Gothic as "decorative."[7] But Walpole's work asks: why is eighteenth-century classicism also not theatrical or decorative? Marble Hill House, for example, is both associational and theatrical; it reminds the viewers and inhabitants of an earlier time and as a scene of riverside retirement becomes a stage set for visitors (fig. 19). In the light of Walpole's argument, it is possible to see the relative absurdity of the neo-Palladians on the one hand importing an idea of Italianate Republic architecture while on the other hand claiming that it is a universal, proportionate, natural form.

The possibility that architectural form is rhetorical, which locates this book's argument as post-Walpole, offers new ways of reconsidering the story about literature and architecture that emerges in this book. In part I have been interested throughout in recent arguments that "by attending to rhetoric in the human sciences, scholars can begin to move away from boundaries and distinctions that characterize disciplinarity."

19. Marble Hill House, London (1724)

But tying architecture to questions of representation implicit in rhetoric raises issues that are in fact specific to architecture as a discipline, especially to architectural representation, which could be described as the site where architectural discipline, practice, and literature, understood rhetorically, meet.[8] When mid-eighteenth-century British architecture begins to reject the proportionate (and the classical) and embraces instead an architecture of participatory viewing, in which viewers use their imagination to recover the historical period of the building, architectural representation interrogates and opposes two principal techniques: the plan and the view. At the same time, these architectural issues also seem to have affected subsequent literary works.

Between 1660 and 1760 architectural representation, and thus architecture as both discipline and practice, was changing. In the seventeenth century "the plan dominated architecture as never before or since."[9] A plan, a stylized map of a building, idealizes the building's orderliness. In its emphasis on idealized order, the plan is similar to and perhaps more fitting for the classical arguments over proportion. As mid-eighteenth-century architecture begins to move beyond proportion, publications begin to rely more on the architectural view, with its assumption of human interaction with the building. Although there is a difference between the "view" and what Robin Evans calls the eighteenth-century "developed surface interior," they share the same interest in expanding the range of what could be seen in an architectural drawing.[10] The view, like the developed surface interior but unlike the plan, values the experience of a space; during Walpole's time it seems, for that reason, to have been considered a more appropriate tool for architectural representation.

Nonetheless, as Alberto Péréz-Goméz and Louise Pelletier have pointed out, "in the eighteenth century, geometric perspective lost its privileged status as a 'symbolic form' describing the order of the world, yet it would be misleading to assume that perspective was abandoned entirely."[11] Robert Adam's *Ruins of the Palace of the Emperor Diocletian*

(1763), for example, features a two-part gatefold engraving; a "Geometrical Elevation of the . . . East Wall of the Palace" on the top is contrasted with an "Elevation of the same wall as it now remains" on the bottom.[12] The second image, by seeming to reveal the passage of time, implies that it more accurately shows the wall as it is and raises the question of which would be a better way of representing the building: the orderly, idealized, "Geometrical" elevation or the disorderly, actual, associational view (fig. 20). Similarly, Joshua Kirby's *The Perspective of Architecture* (1761), consisting entirely of engravings, includes many pages that oppose the plan and the view. Plate 38, for example, includes three different images: a horizontally composed geometric representation of a building, printed above two views of the same building reconsidered in the bottom images as ruins (fig. 21).[13] Not only do these images imply a different, less reductive way of imagining a building as it is, the visual texts of at least these particular architectural publications give the viewer a choice of how to see a

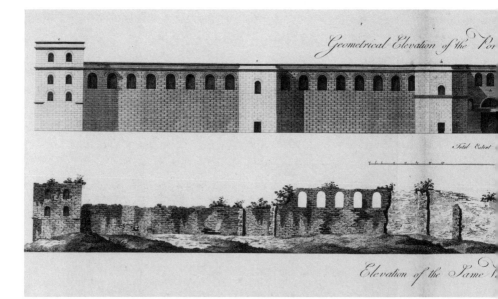

20. Robert Adam, *Ruins of the Palace of the Emperor Diocletian* (1763), plate 10. (Courtesy of Avery

building: plan or view, idealized or experiential. Offering the reader a choice of ways to read a building architecturally indicates a perceived insufficiency of one single representation, or more accurately, one technique for representation.

In *The Castle of Otranto* (and in his *Correspondence*), Walpole seems to have assimilated these changes in architectural representation, as his own concerns about representational convention rely on architectural terms. In the second preface to the novel, for example, Walpole meditates on the rule-bound reduction of thought, considering it (as is so often the case in Britain) in relation to Shakespearean and French theater. Ridiculing the French dislike for Shakespeare, he writes: "Unhappy Shakespeare! hadst thou made Rosencrans inform . . . Guildenstern of the ichnography of the palace of Copenhagen . . . Paris would have . . . adore[d] thy talents" (12). Unlike Shakespeare, Walpole, or by extension, the British, Paris would prefer an ichnography, and an ichnography is a plan;

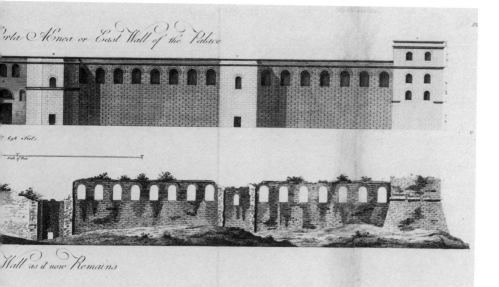

Architectural and Fine Arts Library, Columbia University in the City of New York)

Walpole's sarcastic treatment of the Parisian preference for the architecture of the plan indicates his own rejection of it. A plan, an ichnography, constrains an artist unnaturally, a point he underscores when he describes the best French poetry as "vaulting in spite of . . . fetters" (11). For Walpole, good French poets succeed despite the constraints that the rules—a ground plan, an ichnography—place upon them.

Responding to a visit to one of Capability Brown's parks four years before writing *The Castle of Otranto*, Walpole argues that Brown's landscaping "is full as unnatural as if it was drawn with a rule and compass."[14] Of course, by "rule" Walpole is referring to a straight measuring device, which when used architecturally would create a grid, the precondition for a scale plan. It controls, or as Walpole might say, "fetters," a represen-

21. Joshua Kirby, *The Perspective of Architecture* (1761), plate 38. (Courtesy of Avery Architectural and Fine Arts Library, Columbia University in the City of New York)

tation of the built environment. Without a rule and compass, one cannot draw lines as straight or circles as round as they might be; such figures would be more "associational." They would, in a way, be less rule-bound. And Walpole would have preferred it that way. Although the natural alternative does not emerge, Walpole seems to believe that the park would have been more natural had it been drawn freehand, so to speak.

In this book Walpole's comments come at the seeming end of an argument over the definition of nature, most visible in the controversy over the origins of Stonehenge—moving as they do from Roman, universal, and mathematical to British, local, and rude. By the end of the period, nature is localized and historical, something closer in meaning to native, at the same time that architectural representation moves from the plan to the view. As nature moves from the mathematical to the historical, by the 1740s some British authors and architects had come to believe that the ruins which dotted the countryside, typified by Stonehenge and alluded to in, say, Gray's "Country Churchyard," were more naturally British than Palladianism could be. It would seem, in other words, that changes in understandings of the nation are concomitant with changing understandings of nature. For Gray and others, those specifically British and rural ruins became more important than the imported universalizing standards. What had been a mathematical simplicity, for Milton or Pope, had become, with Gray, rural simplicity (one might even say pastoral, meaning both the supposed simplicity of a pastoral setting and also, punning on the word *pastoral*, the supposed simplicity of the past).

A preference for the British, a retreat to the rural, and the unnaturalness of formal design: as others have noted, these and similar claims lend themselves to a theory of preromanticism, a term so disputed that Marshall Brown, author of a book titled *Preromanticism*, went on to state, in a subsequent book, "To be sure, few scholars still use the term *preromanticism*." And yet there is a sense in which "romanticism comes into its own by recapitulating its prehistory," even if that prehistory is not "preromanticism."[15] It is in part the argument, albeit not the focus, of this book, that the prehistory of romanticism must include a consideration of architectural history and architectural representation, a prehistory into which the author-architects under consideration could provide special access.

Although, given the controversies between Wordsworth and, say, Blake or Byron, it is not possible to consider any one of them an unqualified representative, British romantics do nonetheless share a similar interest in the rhetoric of architecture and vision. Coleridge's "Kubla Khan," for example, subtitled "a vision," is, in addition to the architectural setting of the poem itself, supposed to have been composed in a rural, natural, British setting, "a lonely farm-house between Porlock and Linton, on the Exmoor confines of Somerset and Devonshire." Similarly, Byron wrote "Elegy on Newstead Abbey," which combines a Gray-like title and setting with Walpole's interest in the "gloomth of the abbey"— "pensive shades around thy ruins glide,""more honour'd in thy fall / Than modern mansions in their pillar'd state"—and adds to both the familiar sense of the natural, historicized British countryside: "years roll on years; to ages, ages yield" (4, 5–6, 37). By the time Byron writes that "deformity is daring," in *The Deformed Transformed: A Drama* (1824), interest in fragments of the rude British past have so transformed attitudes toward deformed form that it is no longer exactly daring to appreciate it (line 313).

Wordsworth's "Lines Composed a Few Miles above Tintern Abbey" could, in this way, represent a romantic assimilation of the architectural lessons of the preceding author-architects. As if the setting of the poem at a ruined abbey was not similar enough to a proto-Gothic sensibility, by opposing Tintern's "beauteous forms" (23) to "the dreary intercourse of daily life" (131), the poem ties architectural rhetoric quite specifically to modernity, represented in the poem by "the din / Of towns and cities" (25–26), modernity being one way of figuring the shift from form as space to form as rhetoric. At the same time, the poem relates this shift specifically in the context of the narrator's changing understanding of nature: "For I have learned / To look on nature, not as in the hour / Of thoughtless youth; but hearing oftentimes / The still, sad music of humanity" (88–91). Nature, here humanized, replays the emergence of nature historicized first seen in the 1740s. Moreover, in opposing the narrator's new understanding of nature to a previous one specifically described as being "unborrowed from the eye" (83), the poem replays the argument over architectural representation, from plan to view, correlating with the shift from nature as symmetrical representation of universal order to nature as a participatory experience of fragmentation and disorder: "Of eye, and ear,—both what they half create, / And what perceive" (106–7). Often read as Wordsworth's critique of empiricism, the statement could be seen, in the light of the changes in architectural representation, as a statement of representation's simultaneous perception and creation.

The shared explanatory or representational power of drawing and writing means that they perform similar roles in architecture and literature. It is in the process of putting something onto the page or in words, and sometimes not before that process, that one comes to understand what one thinks. Architect Renzo Piano, for example, contends that "unless you draw something, you do not understand it. It is a mistake to believe that now I understand the problem and now I draw it. Rather, right at the time you draw you realize what problem is and then you can rethink it."[16] Similarly, Calvin O. Schrag defines writing as "at once discovery of self and self-constitution" and reminds us that it "takes place only against the background of a language already spoken, which has both a history and a formal structure."[17] That is, writing and drawing take place against the background of a discipline and a practice, both. Discipline in this context means both the history of a field and the central activity that is presumed to justify the development and/or perception of a semiautonomous practice. In architecture, both meanings of discipline are joined in architectural representation, just as they are joined by persuasive writing in literature.

If architecture is rhetorical, there are a variety—maybe an infinitude—of gestures that can be used strategically for different situations (rather than an iconography of architectural styles, according to which there is classical, Gothic, Shingle, modern, etc.). This rhetorical understanding, then, is not the same as stylistic pluralism; it is not a question of choosing from a preexisting palette. Nor is it tied to some particular type of rhetoric; it is not, for example, a Ciceronian understanding of architecture, although such specifics can matter. (See, for example, Christine Smith's analysis of how Alberti's "concinnitus is related to Classical rhetorical theory.")[18] In that architecture understood rhetorically is a question of strategically shaping space contextually for effects (with the question then being what effects, for whom, and why), it is architecture itself, rather than some approach within it, that becomes a variation on Frampton's "critical regionalism."[19] It is true that with architecture, there is the "existing palette" of building materials. But the materials can play a role in the rhetorical considerations, rather than solely being understood structurally, which is part of why it is so important to consider what Frampton calls "the poetics of construction."[20]

It is not so much a question of choosing whether to be a classicist or a structural rationalist in architecture anymore than it is a question of whether to write as a classicist, modernist, or postmodernist in literature. After Walpole it is possible to see that there are not styles in the usual sense; it is not simply the case, for instance, that Vanbrugh chose a Whiggish style. Rather, what is usually considered style can instead be seen as a strategic, contextual claim, a way of representing. Of course the issue then becomes trying to understand why a particular style has been or maybe should be chosen. But that is no more a problem for architecture than it is for literature.

NOTES

BIBLIOGRAPHY

INDEX

Notes

INTRODUCTION:
ON LITERATURE AND ARCHITECTURE

1. Mitchell, *Picture Theory*, 89.

2. Walpole, *Description of the Villa of Mr. Horace Walpole*, 1, unnumbered preface.

3 . Gutman, "Redesigning Architecture Schools," 89.

4. Boyer and Mitgang, *Building Community*, 85.

5. Rouquet, *Present State of the Arts in England*, 96.

6. De Vries, *Economy of Europe in an Age of Crisis*, 36, 38.

7. Porter, *London*, 131.

8. Ibid., 87.

9. Hoskins, *Making of the English Landscape*, 185.

10. Wilton-Ely, "The Rise of the Professional Architect," 183.

11. Quoted in Kaye, *Development of the Architectural Profession in Britain*, 50.

12. Ackerman, *Distance Points*, 363.

13. Swift, "The History of Vanbrug's House," in *Complete Poems*, 7–8.

14. See the "Chronological Index of Titles and Editions" published in Eileen Harris's *British Architectural Books and Writers*. This figure includes various editions of translations of works by Continental architects (such as Fréart, Palladio, Scamozzi, Serlio, and Vignola), not to mention the assorted "builder's companions" explaining measurement (such as *Description and Use of Joynt-Rule* or *Mensuration Made Easy*, both 1661).

15. Palladio, *First Book of Architecture*, unnumbered preface.

16. Kruft, *History of Architectural Theory*, 232.

17. Wilton-Ely, "The Rise of the Professional Architect," 188.

18. Kruft, *History of Architectural Theory*, 229.

19. Bernard Tschumi, foreword to Ockman, *Architecture Culture*, 11.

20. Le Corbusier, *Toward a New Architecture*, 14.

21. Dutton and Mann, "Modernism, Postmodernism, and Architecture's Social Project," 13.

22. Kaye, *Development of the Architectural Profession in Britain*, 47.

23. Crosbie, "The Schools," 50.

24. Dutton, "*Cultural* Studies and Critical *Pedagogy*," 165.

25. Choay, *Rule and the Model*, 9, 11.

26. Frampton, *Studies in Tectonic Culture*, 11.

27. Lotman, *Universe of the Mind*, 45.

28. Moretti, *Signs Taken for Wonders*, 9.

29. Harries, *Ethical Function of Architecture*, 4.

30. Eisenman, "Misreading," *House of Cards*, 173.

31. Crook, *Dilemma of Style*, 17.

32. Nelson Goodman, "How Buildings Mean," in Goodman and Elgin, *Reconsideration in Philosophy and Other Arts and Sciences*, 32.

33. Philip Johnson, quoted in Games, *Behind the Façade*, 86.

34. Burke, *Philosophy of Literary Form*, 1.

35. Lukács, *Theory of the Novel*, 6; de Man, *Blindness and Insight*, 237. Although we now know that it is very awkward that it should be de Man who would want to emphasize an unresolved conflict, his point is still important: it may be too hopeful to either assume or to argue that a form can ultimately resolve a conflict, or a fundamental dissonance of existence.

36. Jameson, *Political Unconscious*, 99; White, *Content of the Form*.

37. Knapp, *Archetype, Architecture, and the Writer*, x.

38. Jameson, "Is Space Political?" 259.

39. Morris, *Essay in Defense of Ancient Architecture*, 9.

40. Fréart, *Parallel of the Ancient Architecture with the Modern*, 118, unnumbered dedicatory epistle.

41. Palladio, *First Book of Architecture*, unnumbered preface.

42. Lacour, *Lines of Thought*, 1.

1. "Truth . . . Is a Just and Naturall Proportion":
Milton, Wotton, and Renaissance Architectural Theory

1. Addison, *Spectator*, no. 267 (Saturday, Jan. 5, 1712), 2:542.

2. Ibid., no. 417 (Saturday, June 28, 1712), 3:566.

3. Mowl and Earnshaw, *Architecture without Kings*, 68ff., 60.

4. See Barker, "Structural Pattern in *Paradise Lost*"; Condee, *Structure in Milton's*

Poetry; McClung, "The Architectonics of *Paradise Lost*"; Shawcross, "The Balanced Structure of *Paradise Lost*"; Weber, *Construction of* Paradise Lost.

5. Weber, *Construction of* Paradise Lost, xi; Condee, *Structure in Milton's Poetry*, 5.

6. Milton, *Second Defense*, in *Complete Poems and Major Prose*, 838.

7. Pointon, *Milton and English Art*, 174; Barker, "Structural Pattern in *Paradise Lost*," 144.

8. Milton, *Reason of Church Government*, in *Complete Poems and Major Prose*, 643.

9. Milton, *Doctrine and Discipline of Divorce*, ibid., 707, 702.

10. Kerrigan, *Sacred Complex*, ix; Cable, *Carnal Rhetoric*, 1; Bennett, *Reviving Liberty*, 15; Achinstein, *Milton and the Revolutionary Reader*, 23.

11. Milton, *Reason of Church Government*, 645.

12. Milton, *Second Defense*, 838.

13. Milton, *The Ready and Easy Way*, in *Complete Poems and Major Prose*, 884.

14. Milton, *Areopagitica*, ibid., 743.

15. Milton, *Of Education*, ibid., 634.

16. Hersey, *Pythagorean Palaces*, 7.

17. Vitruvius, *De architectura* 2:21 (6.2.1). All Vitruvius quotes come from the Granger edition.

18. Milton, *Reason of Church Government*, 645.

19. Alberti, *On the Art of Building in Ten Books*, 7, 156, 304.

20. See Rykwert, *Dancing Column*, chap. 3, "The Body and the World."

21. Alberti, *On the Art of Building in Ten Books*, 305.

22. Ibid., 7.

23. Ibid.

24. Summerson, *Architecture in Britain*, 156.

25. Wotton, *Elements of Architecture*, unnumbered preface, 53.

26. Ibid., 53–55, 6.

27. Ibid., "78" (actually 85).

28. Milton, *Second Defense*, 828, 829. See also Arthos, *Milton and the Italian Cities*; Masson, *Life of John Milton* 1:792–93.

29. Hill, *Milton and the English Revolution*, 53.

30. Ackerman, *Distance Points*, 363.

31. Milton, *Reason of Church Government*, 667–68.

32. Ibid., 646.

33. See for example Foucault, *Discipline and Punish*; Milton, *Reason of Church Government*, 645, 642–43.

34. Milton, *Reason of Church Government*, 642.

35. Heninger, *Subtext of Form in the English Renaissance*, 59.

36. Milton, *Reason of Church Government*, 642.

37. Milton, *Paradise Lost*, in *Complete Poems and Major Prose*, 3.54–55.

38. Summerson, *Classical Language of Architecture*.

39. Wotton, *Elements of Architecture*, 6.

40. Haskin, *Milton's Burden of Interpretation*, 55.

41. Schindler, *Voice and Crisis*, 45.

42. Hersey, *Pythagorean Palaces*, 20.

43. Fish, "Discovery as Form in *Paradise Lost*," 2.

44. Moyles, *The Text of* Paradise Lost, 21.

45. Milton, *Doctrine and Discipline of Divorce*, 707.

46. Ackerman, *Distance Points*, 373.

47. Fowler, *Triumphal Forms*, ix.

48. See, for example, Cesariano's *De architectura* (1521), in Tzonis and Lefaivre, *Classical Architecture*, 21.

49. See Millon, "The Architectural Theory of Francesco di Giorgio."

50. Tzonis and Lefaivre, *Classical Architecture*, 20.

51. Johnson, "Milton's Epic Style," 71, 72, 77.

52. Wittkower, *Architectural Principles in the Age of Humanism*, 8.

53. Wotton, *Elements of Architecture*, "78" [actually 85], 122.

54 Milton, *Of Education*, 631.

2. "AGAINST THE TOO EXACT OBSERVANCE OF THE RULES": VANBRUGH'S DRAMA AND ARCHITECTURE

1. McCormick, *Playwright as Architect*, 17.

2. Swift, "The History of Vanbrug's House," in *Complete Poems*, 7–8.

3. Whistler, *Imagination of Vanbrugh and His Fellow Artists*, 195.

4. *The Provok'd Wife* was produced 134 times between 1700 and 1729, but John Downes's theater history, *Roscius Anglicanus* (1708), significantly omits any mention of it.

5. Vanbrugh, *Short Vindication*, 72.

6. Ibid., 57.

7. Vanbrugh, *Complete Works* 1:207.

8. See Berkowitz, *Sir John Vanbrugh and the End of Restoration Comedy*; Laura Brown, *English Dramatic Form*; Burns, *Restoration Comedy*; Krutch, *Comedy and Conscience after the Restoration*; Loftis, *Politics of Drama in Augustan England*; Zimbardo, *A Mirror to Nature*.

9. Vanbrugh, *Provok'd Wife* 3.2.64–66.

10. Collier, *Short View of the Immorality and Profaneness of the English Stage*, 127, 231, 228, 140.

11. Ibid., 11.

12. Ibid., unnumbered preface, 107.

13. Vanbrugh, *Short Vindication*, 4.

14. Ibid.

15. Colley Cibber, *Apology*, 172.

16. Vanbrugh to Jacob Tonson, 13 July 1703, *Complete Works* 4:9.

17. Ibid.

18. Quoted in Allen, *Clubs of Augustan London*, 236.

19. Defoe, *Daniel Defoe*, 117.

20. Vanbrugh to Jacob Tonson, 13 July 1703, *Complete Works*, 4:9.

21. Because this is the only architecture book Vanbrugh ever mentions, it is important to consider which edition of Palladio he might have used. In *Sir John Vanbrugh: Architect and Dramatist, 1664–1726*, Laurence Whistler argues that it must be "Martin's edition of all four books" published in 1650, the most recent French edition to include the plan (105), but that edition would have been fifty-three years old by 1703. Of the nearly 400 editions of Palladio listed in the Research Library Information Network, an electronic database of America's research libraries, there is only one French edition published in Amsterdam, where Jacob Tonson made the purchase, before the eighteenth century: Le Muet's *Traité des Cinq Ordres d'Architecture* (1682). And significantly enough, this edition, only the first of Palladio's four books, does not include that book's first eleven chapters, which contain information on such important architectural matters as "What ought to be considered and prepared before you begin to build," "Of Foundations," and "Of . . . Walls."

22. Tavernor, *Palladio and Palladianism*, 103.

23. Leacroft, *Development of the English Playhouse*, 65.

24. On turn-of-the-century theater history generally, and Vanbrugh's Haymarket Theatre specifically, see Milhous, *Thomas Betterton and the Management of Lincoln's Inn Fields*; Milhous and Hume, *Vice Chamberlain Coke's Theatrical Papers*; and Thomas, *Documents in Restoration and Georgian*.

25. Leacroft, *Development of the English Playhouse*, 80.

26. Ibid., 90.

27. Ibid., 102.

28. Colley Cibber, *Apology*, 173.

29. Quoted in Milhous and Hume, *Vice Chamberlain Coke's Theatrical Papers*, 5.

30. Vanbrugh to Jacob Tonson, 29 Nov. 1719, *Complete Works* 4:123.

31. Perrault, *Ordonnance for the Five Kinds of Columns after the Method of the Ancients*, 49, 47; Vanbrugh, *Short Vindication*, 4.

32. Vanbrugh to Jacob Tonson, 13 July 1703, *Complete Works* 4:8.

33. Kerry Downes, *Vanbrugh*, 22.

34. Although it lies outside the scope of this chapter, it is my hope that this reading of Vanbrugh's early work, while not directly concerned with Blenheim Palace, Vanbrugh's most famous production, might nonetheless suggest some of its themes.

35. See also Vanbrugh, "Duchess of Malborough's endorsement," June 11, 1709, *Complete Works* 4:30, in which the duchess writes "this paper has something ridiculous in it to preserve the house."

36. Worsley, "Wicked Woman of Marl," 44.

37. Frances Harris, *Passion for Government*, 213.

3. "The Utmost Grace of Uniformity":
Pope's Anglo-Palladian Epic

1. Pope to Mrs. ——, *Correspondence* 1:432. All references to Pope's correspondence come from Sherburn's edition.

2. Spence, *Observations, Anecdotes, and Characters of Books and Men*, §459, 197.

3. Pope to Swift, 14 Sept. 1725, 2:322.

4. Ackerman, *Villa*, 12, 15.

5. Summerson, "The Classical Country House in 18th-Century England," 552; Pope to Swift, 23 March 1736/37, 4:63.

6. Deutsch, *Resemblance and Disgrace*, 87.

7. Pope to Martha Blount, 15 June 1724, 2:239.

8. Pope to Hugh Bethel, 9 Aug. 1726, 2:386.

9. Ackerman, *Villa*, 214.

10. Lubbock, *Tyranny of Taste*, 55, 61.

11. Deutsch, *Resemblance and Disgrace*, 88; Pope to Judith Cowper, 17 Jan. [1722/23], 2:155.

12. Pope to Swift, Jan. 1727/28, 1:220.

13. Pope to the earl of Oxford, [c. 2 Dec. 1730], 3:153.

14. Pope to Caryll, 19 March 1713/14, 1:220.

15. Laura Brown, *Alexander Pope*, 78. And it is also important that Pope should contend in conversation with Spence that Lord Bolingbroke, to whom *An Essay on Man* is addressed, "in everything has been acting for the good of the public these twenty-five years, and without any view to his own interest" (§276).

16. Cope, *Criteria of Certainty*, 166.

17. Klein, *Shaftesbury and the Culture of Politeness*, 8.

18. Pocock, *Virtue, Commerce, and History*, 236.

19. Pope to Swift, 16 Feb. 1732/33, 3:348.

20. Rogers, *Essays on Pope*, 27.

21. Hutcheson, *Enquiry concerning Beauty, Order, Harmony, Design*, 40.

22. Hersey and Freedman, *Possible Palladian Villas*, 15.

23. Bentman and Müller, *Villa as Hegemonic Architecture*, 29.

24. Brownell, *Pope's Villa*, 5.

25. Pope to Fortescue, 2 Sept. [1731], 3:225.

26. See Spence, *Observations, Anecdotes, and Characters of Books and Men*, §617: "A study should be built [on the] east, as Sir Henry Wotton says in his little piece of architecture."

27. Pope to Walsh, 2 July 1706, 1:19.

28. Morris, *Essay in Defense of Ancient Architecture*, 14.

29. Pocock, *Virtue, Commerce, and History*, 237; Gerrard, *Patriot Opposition to Walpole*, 5.

30. Griffin, *Regaining Paradise*, 169.

31. Doody, *Daring Muse*, 81.

32. Pope, "Essay on Criticism," in *Poems* l. 89.

33. Vanbrugh, *Short Vindication*, 72.

34. Pope, *Essay on Man*, in *Poems*, 1.294.

35. Pope to Lady Mary Wortley Montagu, July 1717, 1:405.

36. Pope to Congreve, 16 Jan. 1714/15, 1:274.

37. Pope to Caryll, July 1717, 1:13.

38. Pope to Lady Mary Wortley Montagu, 18 Aug. [1718], 1:352–53.

39. Dowling, *Epistolary Moment*, 12, 11.

40. Klein, *Shaftesbury and the Culture of Politeness*, 115, 102.

41. Krieger, *Ekphrasis*, 247.

42. Pope, *Essay on Man*, 502.

43. Spence, *Observations, Anecdotes, and Characters*, §395, 637.

44. Ibid., §395, 637.

45. Griffin, *Regaining Paradise*, 66.

46. Tillotson, *On the Poetry of Pope*, 105, 133.

47. Cohen, "Notes on the Teaching of Eighteenth-Century Poetry of Natural Description," 81.

48. Damrosch, *Imaginative World of Alexander Pope*, 268.

49. Barrell, *Birth of Pandora and the Division of Knowledge*, 50.

50. Pope, *Essay on Man*, 502.

51. Krieger, *Ekphrasis*, 248.

52. Kallich, *Heaven's First Law*, 73.

53. Hersey and Freedman, *Possible Palladian Villas*, 16.

54. Foucault, *Madness and Civilization*, ix.

55. Pope, quoted in Tillotson, *On the Poetry of Pope*, 118.

56. Tillotson, *On the Poetry of Pope*, 150.

57. Pope to the earl of Orrery, 20 Dec. 1738, 4:154.

58. Pope to Warburton, 11 April [1739], 4:171.

59. Warburton, *Vindication of Mr. Pope's* Essay on Man, 4, 6.

4. "Approach and Read . . . the Stone":
Toward An Archaeology of Gray's *Elegy*

1. Stukely, *Itinerarum Curiosum*, 3, 2.

2. See, for example, Stukely, *Stonehenge*; Wood, *Origin of Building*; Langley, *Ancient Architecture Restored*; Langley, *Gothick Architecture*; Wood, *Choir Gaure vulgarly called Stonehenge*; Morris, *Rural architecture in the Gothick Taste*.

3. Stukely, *Stonehenge*, 5.

4. Rykwert, *First Moderns*, 130.

5. Gray, "Elegy Written in a Country Churchyard," *Poems of Gray, Collins, and Goldsmith*, 115–16. All references to the "Elegy" come from the Lonsdale edition.

I use the term *archaeology* advisedly, realizing that the authors I survey did not use the term themselves. In using *archaeology*, I intend to refer to the actual activity which we today call archaeology, that is, related field-based techniques for researching the past, research based more on excavation and examination than on written records. Moreover, I am also incorporating the use Michel Foucault made of the idea of archaeology. For him, archaeology provides a model with which to address the question of "how . . . one [is] to specify the different concepts that enable us to conceive of discontinuity (threshold, rupture, break, mutation, transformation)" (*Archaeology of Knowledge*, 5), precisely the question I hope this interdisciplinary reading of the *Elegy* might begin to answer.

6. Pigott, *Ancient Britons and the Antiquarian Imagination*, 29.

7. See, for example, Jack, "Gray's *Elegy* Reconsidered"; Brady, "Structure and Meaning in Gray's *Elegy*"; Marshall Brown, *Preromanticism*.

8. Quoted in Chippindale, *Stonehenge Complete*, 46.

9. Evelyn, 22 July 1654, *Diary and Correspondence* 1.310.

10. Pepys, 15 June 1668, *Shorter Pepys*, 923, 927.

11. Gray, "Journal in the Lakes," *Works* 1:260.

12. Jones, *Most Notable Antiquity of Great Britain, Vulgarly called Stone-heng*, 43.

13. Ibid., 5, 43, 8.

14. Wittkower, *Palladio and English Palladianism*, 63.

15. Chippindale, *Stonehenge Complete*, 57.

16. Charleton, *Chorea Gigantum*, 9, unnumbered dedicatory epistle.

17. Chippindale, *Stonehenge Complete*, 47.

18. Kroll, *Material Word*, 34.

19. Webb, *Vindication of* Stone-Heng Restored, 4.

20. Aubrey, *Monumenta Britannica*, 26, 32, 128.

21. Defoe, *Tour* 1:196, 1:198.

22. Chippindale, *Stonehenge Complete*, 71.

23. Weinbrot, "Gray's 'Progress of Poesy' and 'The Bard,'" 313.

24. Aubrey, *Monumenta Britannica*, 128.

25. Stukely, *Stonehenge*, 5, 11, 12.

26. Ibid., 5.

27. Wood, *Choir Gaure vulgarly called Stonehenge*, 64.

28. Varey, *Space and the Eighteenth Century Novel*, 98, 99.

29. Langley, *Ancient Architecture Restored*, unnumbered dedicatory epistle.

30. Langley, *Gothick Architecture*, last plate.

31. Venuti, *Description of the first discoveries of the ancient city of Herclea*, 52.

32. Krauss, *Pompeii and Herculaneum*, 119.

33. Deiss, *Herculaneum*, 37.

34. Gray to Mrs. Gray, [14] June 1740, *Correspondence* 1:164. All references to Gray's correspondence come from the Toynbee and Whibley edition.

35. Deiss, *Herculaneum*, 37.

36. Venuti, *Description of the first discoveries of the ancient city of Herclea*, 101.

37. Gray to West, [8] April [1742], 1:192.

38. Gray to Chute and Mann, [1742?], 1:215.

39. Gray, "Essay on Norman Architecture," *Works*, 1:295, 301.

40. Gray, "Observations on English Metre," *Gray's Poems*, 327.

41. Gray, "Some Remarks on the Poems of Sir John Lydgate," ibid., 372, 369.

42. Sitter, "The Flight from History in Mid Eighteenth-Century Poetry (and Twentieth Century Criticism)," 98.

43. Gray to Mason, [c. Dec. 1751], 1:359.

44. Gray, "Observations on English Metre," *Gray's Poems*, 331.

45. Rykwert, *On Adam's House in Paradise*, 82.

46. Brooks, "Gray's Storied Urn," 23.

47. Gray to Dodsley, 12 Feb. [1753], 1:371.

48. Quoted in Epstein, "Professing Gray," 91.

49. In his introduction to Gray's *Elegy* in *Poems of Gray, Collins, and Goldsmith*, Roger Lonsdale makes a similar point regarding the poem as a whole: "The figure of the Poet

is no longer the urbane, worldly, rational Augustan man among men, with his own place in society; what G. dramatizes is the poet as outside, with an uneasy consciousness of a sensibility and imagination at once unique and burdensome" (115).

50. Guillory, *Cultural Capital*, 114.

51. Jestin, *Answer to the Lyre*, 206.

5. "To Invent in Art and Folly": Walpole's Castle of Otranto

1. Walpole to Mrs. Archibald Allison, 18 Feb. 1790, *Correspondence* 42:274–75. Unless otherwise indicated, all references to Walpole's correspondence come from the Lewis edition.

2. Walpole to Chute, 5 Aug. 1771, 35:127.

3. Walpole, *Anecdotes of Painting in England*, 119.

4. Walpole to Mrs. Archibald Allison, 18 Feb. 1790, 42:274.

5. Walpole to Sir Horace Mann, 27 April 1753, 20:372.

6. John Archer, "The Beginnings of Association in British Architectural Esthetics," 241, 246.

7. Harbison, *The Built, the Unbuilt, and the Unbuildable*, 99.

8. Quoted in Crook, *The Dilemma of Style*, 45.

9. Sloterdijk, *Critique of Cynical Reason*, 5.

10. Walpole to Michael Lort, 27 July 1789, 16:221.

11. Walpole to William Bewley, 23 May 1778, 16:131.

12. Walpole, *Castle of Otranto*, 12. All references to this novel come from the Lewis edition.

13. Ames, "Strawberry Hill," 352.

14. Considering *The Castle of Otranto* in architectural terms suggests how much has changed, aesthetically, in the approximately one hundred years since Milton's *Paradise Lost*. In *Contested Castle*, Kate Ferguson Ellis describes *The Castle of Otranto* as a "Gothic revision of the myth of the fall" (57).

15. This could seem to be an anachronistic use of the word folly; the *OED*, for example, dates the first architectural use of the word after Walpole's death. But there are earlier instances of the word *folly* being used architecturally. For example, Andrew Marvell's poem "Upon Appleton House" (1681) claims: "But sure those buildings last not long, / Founded by folly, kept by wrong" (st. 28). And Lawrence Sterne's *Life and Opinions of Tristram Shandy* refers to "the scaffold work of INSTRUCTION, its true point of folly, without the BUILDING behind it" (384).

16. Headley and Meulenkamp,, xxii, xxiii.

17. Walpole to Anne Pitt, 19 Jan. 1766, 31:99; Walpole to Mann, 8 June 1771, 23:312.

18. Quoted in Clark, *Gothic Revival*, 125.

19. Walpole to Chute, 4 Aug. 1753, 35:76.

20. Walpole to George Montagu, 22 Oct. 1766, 10:232.

21. See, for example, Over, *Ornamental Architecture in the Gothic, Chinese and Modern Taste*; Decker, *Gothic Architecture Decorated*; Overton, *Temple Builders Most Useful Companion*; Rawlins, *Familiar Architecture*; Wrighte, *Grotesque Architecture*.

22. Burke, *Philosophical Enquiry*, 101.

23. Walpole to Mann, 25 Feb. 1750, 20:127.

24. Vitruvius, *De architectura*, 2.1.4; Alberti, *On the Art of Building in Ten Books*, 303, 309; Wotton, *Elements of Architecture*, 21.

25. Burke, *Philosophical Enquiry*, 100, 99.

26. Ponte, "Architecture and Phallocentrism in Richard Payne Knight's Theory," 274.

27. Vidler, *Architectural Uncanny*, 71.

28. Bernard Tschumi, "Broadway Follies," in Archer and Vidler, *Follies*, 42.

29. Tschumi, "Madness and the Combinative," 152.

30. Rawlins, *Familiar Architecture*, ii.

31. John Archer, "The Beginnings of Association in British Architectural Aesthetics," 253.

32. Walpole to Richard Bentley, Sept. 1753, 35:148.

33. Quoted in Jackson-Stops, *Fashioning and Functioning of the British Country House*, 386.

34. Seeley, *Description of the Gardens of the Lord Viscount Cobham at Stow*, 125, 124.

35. Quoted in McCarthy, *Origins of the Gothic Revival*, 14.

36. Walpole to Mann, 19 Jan. 1750, 20:111.

37. Ibid., 4 March 1753, 20:361–62.

38. Bryant, "Villa Views and the Uninvited Audience," 16.

39. Mowl, *Horace Walpole*, 143.

40. Eastlake, *History of the Gothic Revival*, 47–48.

41. Walpole to Warton, 21 Aug. 1762, 40:254.

42. Walpole, *Description of the Villa of Mr. Horace Walpole*, unnumbered preface.

43. Walpole to William Cole, 9 March 1765, 1:88.

44. Walpole to Mann, 20 Dec. 1764, 22:270.

45. William Mason to Walpole, 38:6.

46. Quoted in Sabor, *Horace Walpole*, 72.

47. Wrighte, *Grotesque Architecture*.

Coda: On Literary and Architectural Form

1. Worsley, *Classical Architecture in Britain*, xi.

2. Gelertner, *Sources of Architectural Form*, 3, 7, 11, 14.

3. Ibid., 8.

4. Conrads, *Programs and Manifestoes on 20th-Century Architecture*, 74.

5. Moretti, *Signs Taken for Wonders*, 9.

6. See Frampton, "Towards a Critical Regionalism."

7. Worsley, *Classical Architecture in Britain*, 195.

8. Messer-Davidow, Shumway, and Sylvan, Foreword, x. See also, for instance, Bernard-Donals and Glejzer, *Rhetoric in an Antifoundational World*. In *The Rise and Fall of English*, Robert Scholes contends that "now, and the signs of it are everywhere, the pendulum is swinging back to rhetoric" (20).

9. Ackerman, *Distance Points*, 373.

10. Evans, "The Developed Surface," 202.

11. Péréz Goméz and Pelletier, *Architectural Representation and the Perspective Hinge*, 215.

12. Adam, *Ruins of the Palace of the Emperor Diocletian at Spalato in Dalmation*, plate 10.

13. Thomas Major's *The Ruins of Paestum, otherwise Posidonia, in Magna Graecia* shows the buildings as ruins, as they are, not as they were, not an elevation or a plan, but a view. Adam, Kirby, and Major were all in Walpole's library, according to Allen T. Hazen's *A Catalogue of Walpole's Library* (who also states that the Major volume is "a subscription copy").

14. Walpole to Montagu, 4 July 1760, 9:285.

15. Marshall Brown, *Turning Points*, 199, 213.

16. Piano, "The Building Workshop," 127.

17. Schrag, *Self after Postmodernity*, 16.

18. Smith, *Architecture in the Culture of Early Humanism*, 98.

19. See Frampton, "Towards a Critical Regionalism."

20. Frampton, *Studies in Tectonic Culture*.

Bibliography

Achinstein, Sharon. *Milton and the Revolutionary Reader*. Princeton: Princeton Univ. Press, 1994.

Ackerman, James. *Distance Points: Essays in Theory and Renaissance Art and Architecture*. Cambridge: MIT Press, 1991.

———. *The Villa: Form and Ideology of a Country House*. Princeton: Princeton Univ. Press, 1990.

Adam, Robert. *Ruins of the Palace of the Emperor Diocletian at Spalato in Dalmation*. London, 1763.

Addison, Joseph. *The Spectator*. 5 vols. Ed. Donald F. Bond. New York: Oxford Univ. Press, 1965.

Alberti, Leon Battista. *On the Art of Building in Ten Books*. Trans. Joseph Rykwert, Neil Leach, and Robert Tavernor. Cambridge: MIT Press, 1988.

Allen, Robert J. *The Clubs of Augustan London*. Hamden, CT: Archon, 1967.

Ames, Dianne S. "Strawberry Hill: Architecture of the 'As If.'" *Studies in Eighteenth-Century Culture* 8 (1979): 351–63.

Archer, B. J., and Anthony Vidler. *Follies: An Architecture for the Late-Twentieth-Century Landscape. An Exhibition at Leo Castelli Gallery, New York, James Corcoran Gallery, Los Angeles*. New York: Rizzoli, 1983.

Archer, John. "The Beginnings of Association in British Architectural Aesthetics." *ECS* 16:3 (Spring 1983): 241–64.

Arthos, John. *Milton and the Italian Cities*. New York: Barnes and Noble, 1968.

Aubrey, John. *Monumenta Britannica, or A Miscellany of British Antiquities*. 1665–95. Eds. John Fowles and Rodney Legg. Dorset: Dorset Publishing Co, 1980.

Barker, Arthur E. "Structural Pattern in *Paradise Lost*." In *Milton: Modern Essays in Criticism*. Ed. Arthur E. Barker, 142–55. New York: Oxford Univ. Press, 1965.

Barrell, John. *The Birth of Pandora and the Division of Knowledge*. Houndsmill: Macmillan, 1992.

Bennett, Joan. *Reviving Liberty: Radical Christian Humanism in Milton's Great Poems*. Cambridge: Harvard Univ. Press, 1989.

Bentmann, Richard, and Michael Müller. *The Villa as Hegemonic Architecture.* Trans. Tim Spence and David Craven. Atlantic Highlands, NJ: Humanities Press, 1992.

Berkowitz, Gerald. *Sir John Vanbrugh and the End of Restoration Comedy.* Costerus 31. Amsterdam: Editions Rodopi, 1981.

Bernard-Donals, Michael, and Richard Glejzer. *Rhetoric in an Antifoundational World: Language, Culture, and Pedagogy.* New Haven: Yale Univ. Press, 1998.

Boyer, Ernest L., and Lee D. Mitgang. *Building Community: A New Future for Architecture Education and Practice.* Princeton: Carnegie Foundation for the Advancement of Teaching, 1996.

Brady, Frank. "Structure and Meaning in Gray's Elegy." In *From Sensibility to Romanticism: Essays Presented to Frederick A. Pottle.* Ed. Frederick W. Hilles and Harold Bloom, 177–89. New York: Oxford Univ. Press, 1965.

Brooks, Cleanth. "Gray's Storied Urn." In *Twentieth Century Interpretations of Gray's* Elegy: *A Collection of Critical Essays.* Ed. Herbert W. Starr, 23–32. Englewood Cliffs, NJ: Prentice-Hall, 1968.

Brown, Laura. *Alexander Pope.* Oxford: Blackwell, 1985.

———. *English Dramatic Form, 1660–1760.* New Haven: Yale Univ. Press, 1981.

Brown, Marshall. *Preromanticism.* Baltimore: Johns Hopkins Univ. Press, 1992.

———. *Turning Points: Essays in the History of Cultural Expressions.* Stanford: Stanford Univ. Press, 1997.

Brownell, Morris R. *Alexander Pope and the Arts of Georgian England.* Oxford: Oxford Univ. Press, 1978.

———. *Pope's Villa: Views of Pope's Villa, Grotto, and Garden: a Microcosm of English Landscape.* London: GLC, 1980.

Bryant, Julius. "Villa Views and the Uninvited Audience." In *The Georgian Villa.* Ed. Dana Arnold, 11–24. London: Alan Sutton, 1996.

Burke, Edmund. *A Philosophical Enquiry into the Origin of our Ideas of the Sublime and Beautiful.* 1757. Ed. James T. Boulton. South Bend: Univ. of Notre Dame Press, 1968.

Burke, Kenneth. *The Philosophy of Literary Form: Studies in Symbolic Action.* 2d ed. Baton Rouge: Louisiana State Univ. Press, 1967.

Burns, Edward. *Restoration Comedy: Crises of Desire and Identity.* Houndmills: MacMillan, 1987.

Cable, Lana. *Carnal Rhetoric: Milton's Iconoclasm and the Poetics of Desire.* Durham: Duke Univ. Press, 1995.

Campbell, Colen. *Vitruvius Britannicus, or The British Architect, Containing The Plans, Elevations, and Sections of the Regular Buildings, both Publick and Private, in Great Britain, with a variety of new Designs; in 200 large Folio Plates, Engraven by the best Hands, and Drawn either from the Buildings themselves, or the Original Designs of the Architects.* London, 1715.

Charleton, Walter, M.D. *Chorea Gigantum: Or, The Most Famous Antiquity of Great Britain, vulgarly called Stonehenge, standing on Salisbury Plain, Restored to the Danes.* 2d ed. London, 1725.

Chippindale, Christopher. *Stonehenge Complete.* New York: Thames and Hudson, 1983.

Choay, Françoise. *The Rule and the Model: On the Theory of Architecture and Urbanism.* Ed. Denise Bratton. Cambridge: MIT Press, 1997.

Cibber, Colley. *An Apology for the Life of Colley Cibber.* Ed. with an introduction by B. R. S. Fone. Ann Arbor: Univ. of Michigan Press, 1968.

Clark, Kenneth. *Gothic Revival: An Essay in the History of Taste.* Rev. ed. New York: Scribner's, 1950.

Cohen, Ralph. "Notes on the Teaching of Eighteenth-Century Poetry of Natural Description." In *Teaching Eighteenth-Century Poetry.* Ed. Christopher Fox, 75–102. New York: AMS Press, 1990.

Collier, Jeremy. *A Short View of the Immorality and Profaneness of the English Stage: Together with the Sense of Antiquity Upon this Argument.* London, 1698.

Colomina, Beatriz, ed. *Sexuality and Space.* New York: Princeton Architectural Press, 1992.

Condee, Ralph Waterbury. *Structure in Milton's Poetry: From the Foundation to the Pinnacles.* University Park: Pennsylvania State Univ. Press, 1974.

Conrads, Ulrich. *Programs and Manifestoes on 20th-Century Architecture.* Cambridge: MIT Press, 1970.

Cope, Jackson. *The Metaphoric Structure of Paradise Lost.* Baltimore: Johns Hopkins Univ. Press, 1962.

Cope, Kevin L. *Criteria of Certainty: Truth and Judgment in the English Enlightenment.* Lexington: Univ. of Kentucky Press, 1990.

Crook, J. Mordaunt. *The Dilemma of Style: Architectural Ideas from the Picturesque to the Post-Modern.* Chicago: Univ. of Chicago Press, 1987.

Crosbie, Michael J. "The Schools: How They're Failing the Profession (And What We Can Do about It)." *Progressive Architecture* 75 (Sept. 1995): 47–51, 94, 96.

Damrosch, Leopold, Jr. *The Imaginative World of Alexander Pope.* Berkeley: Univ. of California Press, 1987.

Decker, Paul. *Gothic Architecture Decorated. Consisting of a Large Collection of Temples, Banqueting, Summer and Green Houses; Gazebo's Alcoves; Faced Garden, and Umbrello'd Seats; Terminari's, and Rustic Garden Seats, Out Houses, and Hermitages for Summer and Winter, Obelisks, Pyramids, &c. Many of which may be executed with Pollards, Rude Branches and Roots of Trees. Being a Taste entirely NEW.* London, 1759.

Defoe, Daniel. *Daniel Defoe.* Ed. J. T. Boulton. New York: Schocken, 1965.

———. *A Tour through the Whole Island of Great Britain.* Ed. D.C. Browning. 2 vols. New York: Dent, 1962.

Deiss, Joseph Jay. *Herculaneum: Italy's Buried Treasure.* Rev. ed. New York: Harper & Row, 1985.

Deitz, Paula. "Painshill Park, Surrey." *Antiques* 139 (June 1991): 1118–29.

de Man, Paul. *Blindness and Insight: Essays in the Rhetoric of Contemporary Criticism.* 2d ed. Minneapolis: Univ. of Minnesota Press, 1983.

Deutsch, Helen. *Resemblance and Disgrace: Alexander Pope and the Deformation of Culture.* Cambridge: Harvard Univ. Press, 1996.

De Vries, Jan. *The Economy of Europe in an Age of Crisis, 1600–1750.* New York: Cambridge Univ. Press, 1976.

———. *European Urbanization, 1500–1800.* Cambridge: Harvard Univ. Press, 1984.

Doody, Margaret. *The Daring Muse: Augustan Poetry Reconsidered.* New York: Cambridge Univ. Press, 1985.

Dowling, William C. *The Epistolary Moment: The Poetics of the Eighteenth-Century Verse Epistle.* Princeton: Princeton Univ. Press, 1991.

Downes, John. *Roscius Anglicanus, or an Historical Review of the Stage: After it had been suppress'd by means of the late Unhappy Civil War, begun in 1641, till the time of King Charles IIs. Restoration in May 1660. Giving an Account of its Rise again; of the time and Places the Governours of both the Companies first Erected their Theaters.* 1708. Ed. Judith Milhous and Robert D. Hume. London: Society for Theater Research, 1987.

Downes, Kerry. *English Baroque Architecture.* London: A. Zwemmer, 1966.

———. *Sir John Vanbrugh: A Biography.* London: Sigwick & Jackson, 1987.

———. *Vanbrugh.* London: A. Zwemmer, 1977.

Dryden, John. "To My Honour'd Friend *Dr. Charleton,* on his learned and useful Works; and more particularly this of Stone-heng, by him Restored to the true Founders." In Walter Charleton, M.D. *Chorea Gigantum.* 2d ed. London, 1725.

Dutton, Thomas A. "*Cultural* Studies and Critical *Pedagogy: Cultural Pedagogy* and Architecture." In *Reconstructing Architecture: Critical Discourse and Social Practices.* Ed. Thomas A. Dutton and Lian Hurst Mann, 158–201. Minneapolis: Univ. of Minnesota Press, 1996.

Dutton, Thomas A., and Lian Hurst Mann. "Modernism, Postmodernism, and Architecture's Social Project." Introduction to *Reconstructing Architecture: Critical Discourse and Social Practices.* Ed. Thomas A. Dutton and Lian Hurst Mann, 1–25. Minneapolis: Univ. of Minnesota Press, 1996.

Eastlake, Charles E. *A History of the Gothic Revival.* 1872. Reprint, New York: American Life Federation, 1975.

Eisenman, Peter, Rosalind Krauss, and Manfredo Tafuri. *House of Cards: Critical Essays.* New York: Oxford Univ. Press, 1987.

Ellis, Kate Ferguson. *The Contested Castle: Gothic Novels and the Subversion of Domestic Ideology*. Urbana: Univ. of Illinois Press, 1989.

Epstein, William H. "Professing Gray: The Resumption of Authority in Eighteenth-Century Studies." In *The Profession of Eighteenth Century Literature: Reflections on an Institution*. Ed. Leo Damrosch, 81–94. Madison: Univ. of Wisconsin Press, 1992.

Evans, Robin. *Translations from Drawing to Building and Other Essays*. London: Architectural Association, 1997.

Evelyn, John. *The Diary and Correspondence of John Evelyn*. Ed. William Bray. London: Bell and Daldy, 1872.

Fish, Stanley. "Discovery as Form in *Paradise Lost*." In *New Essays on Paradise Lost*. Ed. Thomas Kranidas, 1–14. Berkeley: Univ. of California Press, 1969.

Foucault, Michel. *The Archaeology of Knowledge and the Discourse on Language*. Trans. Rupert Swyer. New York: Pantheon, 1972.

———. *Discipline and Punish: The Birth of the Prison*. New York: Vintage Books, 1979.

———. *Madness and Civilization: A History of Insanity in the Age of Reason*. New York: Vintage, 1965.

Fowler, Alastair. *Triumphal Forms: Structural Patterns in Elizabethan Poetry*. Cambridge: Cambridge Univ. Press, 1970.

Frampton, Kenneth. *Studies in Tectonic Culture: The Poetics of Construction in Nineteenth and Twentieth Century Architecture*. Ed. John Cava. Cambridge: MIT Press, 1995.

———. "Towards a Critical Regionalism: Six Points for an Architecture of Resistance." In *The Anti-Aesthetic: Essays on Postmodern Culture*, 16–30. Ed. Hal Foster. Port Townsend, WA: Bay Press, 1983.

Fréart, Roland. *A Parallel of the Ancient Architecture with the Modern, in a collection of the Principal Authors who have written upon the Five Orders*. Trans. John Evelyn. London, 1664.

French, J. Milton. *Life Records of John Milton*. 2 vols. New Brunswick: Rutgers Univ. Press, 1949.

Games, Stephen. *Behind the Façade*. New York: Universe Books, 1986.

Gelertner, Mark. *Sources of Architectural Form: A Critical History of Western Design Theory*. Manchester: Manchester Univ. Press, 1995.

Gerrard, Christine. *The Patriot Opposition to Walpole: Politics, Poetry, and National Myth, 1725–1742*. Oxford: Clarendon Press, 1994.

Ghirardo, Diane. "The Architecture of Deceit." In *Theorizing a New Agenda for Architecture: An Anthology of Architectural Theory, 1965–1995*. Ed. Kate Nesbitt, 386–91. New York: Princeton Architectural Press, 1996.

Gibbs, James. *A Book of Architecture, containing Designs of buildings and ornaments*. London, 1728.

———. *Rules for drawing the several parts of Architecture, in a more exact and easy manner than has been heretofore practised, by which all FRACTIONS, in dividing the principal MEMBERS and their Parts are avoided.* London, 1732.

———. *A Short Accompt of Mr James Gibbs, Architect and of several things he built in England &c. after his return from Italy.* MS 1714, 1753. London: Soane Museum, 1963. Microfilm.

Goodman, Nelson, and Catherine Z. Elgin. *Reconsideration in Philosophy and Other Arts and Sciences.* Indianapolis: Hackett & Co., 1988.

Gray, Thomas. *Correspondence of Thomas Gray.* Ed. Paget Toynbee and Leonard Whibley. 3 vols. Oxford: Clarendon Press, 1936.

———. *Gray's Poems, Letters, and Essays.* Ed. John Drinkwater and Lewis Gibbs. New York: Everyman, 1970.

———. *The Poems of Thomas Gray, William Collins, and Oliver Goldsmith.* Ed. Roger Lonsdale. New York: Norton, 1972.

———. *Works of Thomas Gray in Prose and Verse.* Ed. Edmund Gosse. 4 vols. Providence, RI, 1885.

Griffin, Dustin. *Regaining Paradise: Milton and the Eighteenth Century.* New York: Cambridge Univ. Press, 1986.

Guillory, John. *Cultural Capital: The Problem of Literary Canon Formation.* Chicago: Univ. of Chicago Press, 1993.

Gutman, Robert. "Redesigning Architecture Schools." *Architecture* 85:8 (Aug. 1996): 87–89.

Harbison, Robert. *The Built, the Unbuilt, and the Unbuildable: In Pursuit of Architectural Meaning.* New York: Thames and Hudson, 1991.

Harries, Karsten. *The Ethical Function of Architecture.* Cambridge: MIT Press, 1997.

Harris, Eileen. *British Architectural Books and Writers, 1556–1785.* Cambridge: Cambridge Univ. Press, 1990.

Harris, Frances. *A Passion for Government: The Life of Sarah, Duchess of Marlborough.* Oxford: Clarendon Press, 1991.

Hartoonian, Gevork. *Ontology of Construction: On Nihilism in Theories of Modern Architecture.* New York: Cambridge Univ. Press, 1994.

Haskin, Dayton. *Milton's Burden of Interpretation.* Philadelphia: Univ. of Pennsylvania Press, 1994.

Havens, Raymond Dexter. *The Influence of Milton on English Poetry.* New York: Russell & Russell, 1961.

Hazen, Allen T. *A Catalogue of Walpole's Library.* New Haven: Yale Univ. Press, 1969.

Headley, Gwyn, and Wim Meulenkamp. *Follies: A National Trust Guide.* London: Jonathan Cape, 1986.

Heninger, S. K., Jr. *The Subtext of Form in the English Renaissance: Proportion Poetical.* University Park: Pennsylvania State Univ. Press, 1994.

Hersey, George. *Pythagorean Palaces: Magic and Architecture in the Italian Renaissance.* Ithaca: Cornell Univ. Press, 1981.

Hersey, George, and Richard Freedman. *Possible Palladian Villas (Plus a Few Instructively Impossible Ones).* Cambridge: MIT Press, 1992.

Heydenreich, Ludwig H., and Wolfgang Lotz. *Architecture in Italy, 1400–1600.* London: Penguin, 1974.

Hill, Christopher. *Milton and the English Revolution.* New York: Viking, 1978.

Hoskins, W. G. *The Making of the English Landscape.* Baltimore: Penguin, 1970.

Hutcheson, Francis. *An Enquiry concerning Beauty, Order, Harmony, Design.* Ed. Peter Kivy. The Hague: Matinus Nijhoof, 1973.

Jack, Ian. "Gray's *Elegy* Reconsidered." In *From Sensibility to Romanticism: Essays Presented to Frederick A. Pottle.* Ed. Frederick W. Hilles and Harold Bloom, 139–69. New York: Oxford Univ. Press, 1965.

Jackson-Stops, Gervase. *The Fashioning and Functioning of the British Country House.* Washington, DC: National Gallery of Art, 1989.

Jameson, Fredric. "Is Space Political?" In *Rethinking Architecture: A Reader in Cultural Theory,* 255–69. New York: Routledge, 1997.

———. *The Political Unconscious: Narrative as a Socially Symbolically Act.* Ithaca: Cornell Univ. Press, 1981.

Jestin, Loftus. *The Answer to the Lyre: Richard Bentley's Illustrations for Thomas Gray's Poems.* Philadelphia: Univ. of Pennsylvania Press, 1990.

Johnson, Lee M. "Milton's Epic Style: the Invocations in Paradise Lost." In *The Cambridge Companion to Milton.* Ed. Dennis Danielson, 65–78. New York: Cambridge Univ. Press, 1989.

Jones, Inigo. *The Most Notable Antiquity of Great Britain, Vulgarly called Stone–Heng, on Salisbury Plain, Restored.* 2d ed. London, 1725.

Kallich, Martin. *Heaven's First Law: Rhetoric and Order in Pope's Essay on Man.* Dekalb: Northern Illinois Univ. Press, 1967.

Karatani, Kojin. *Architecture as Metaphor: Language, Number, Money.* Trans. Sabu Kohso. Ed. Michael Speaks. Cambridge: MIT Press, 1995.

Kaye, Barrington. *The Development of the Architectural Profession in Britain: A Sociological Study.* London: Allen & Unwin, 1960.

Kerrigan, William. *The Sacred Complex: On the Psychogenesis of Paradise Lost.* Cambridge: Harvard Univ. Press, 1983.

Kirby, Joshua. *The Perspective of Architecture.* London, 1761.

Klein, Lawrence E. *Shaftesbury and the Culture of Politeness: Moral Discourse and Cultural*

Politics in Early Eighteenth-Century England. New York: Cambridge Univ. Press, 1994.

Knapp, Bettina L. *Archetype, Architecture, and the Writer*. Bloomington: Indiana Univ. Press, 1986.

Krauss, Theodor. *Pompeii and Herculaneum: The Living Cities of the Dead*. Trans. Robert Erich Wolff. New York: Abrams, 1975.

Krieger, Murray. *Ekphrasis: The Illusion of the Natural Sign*. 2d ed. Baltimore: Johns Hopkins Univ. Press, 1992.

Kroll, Richard. *The Material Word: Literate Culture in the Restoration and Early Eighteenth Century*. Baltimore: Johns Hopkins Univ. Press, 1991.

Kruft, Hanno-Walter. *A History of Architectural Theory: From Vitruvius to the Present*. New York: Zwemmer/Princeton Architectural Press, 1994.

Krutch, Joseph Wood. *Comedy and Conscience after the Restoration*. New York: Columbia Univ. Press, 1949.

Lacour, Claudia Brodsky. *Lines of Thought: Discourse, Architectonics, and the Origin of Modern Philosophy*. Durham: Duke Univ. Press, 1996.

Langley, Batty. *Gothick Architecture, Improved by Rules and Proportions. In many grand designs, of columns, doors, windows, chimney-pieces, arcades, colonnades, porticos, umbrellos, temples, and pavillions, etc. With plans, elevations, and profiles; geometrically explained*. London, 1742.

———. *Practical geometry applied to the useful arts of building . . . calculated for the service of gentlemen as well as artisans*. London, 1726.

———. *A sure guide to builders: or the principles and practice of architecture geometrically demonstrated and made easy*. London, 1729.

Langley, Batty and Thomas. *Ancient Architecture Restored, and Improved, by a Great Variety of Grand and Usefull Designs. Entirely New in the Gothick Mode for the Ornamenting of Buildings and Gardens*. London, 1742.

Leacroft, Richard. *The Development of the English Playhouse*. Ithaca: Cornell Univ. Press, 1973.

Le Corbusier. *Toward a New Architecture*. Trans. Frederick Etchells. 1927. Reprint, New York: Holt, Rinehart, and Winston, 1982.

Le Muet. *Traité des Cinq Ordres d'Architecture dont se sont servi les Ancients. Traduit du Palladio. Augmenté de Nouvelles Inventions Pour l'art de bien bastir*. Edition nouvelle, revüe & corrigé. Amsterdam, 1682.

Levine, William. "From the Ridiculous to the Sublime: Gray's Transvaluation of Pope's Poetics." *Philological Quarterly* 70:3 (Summer 1991): 289–309.

Loftis, John. *The Politics of Drama in Augustan England*. Oxford: Clarendon Press, 1963.

Lotman, Yuri M. *Universe of the Mind: A Semiotic Theory of Culture*. Trans. Ann Shukman.

With an introduction by Umberto Eco. Bloomington: Indiana Univ. Press, 1990.

Lubbock, Jules. *The Tyranny of Taste: The Politics of Architecture and Design in Britain, 1550–1950.* New Haven: Yale Univ. Press, 1995.

Lukács, Georg. *The Theory of the Novel: A Historico-Philosophico Essay on the Forms of Great Epic Literature.* Trans. Anna Bostock. Cambridge: MIT Press, 1971.

Major, Thomas. *The Ruins of Paestum, otherwise Posidonia, in Magna Graecia.* London, 1768.

Martin, Peter. *Pursuing Innocent Pleasures: The Gardening World of Alexander Pope.* Hamden, CT: Archon Books, 1984.

Masson, David. *The Life of John Milton.* 1859–94. Reprint, New York: Peter Smith, 1946.

McCarthy, Michael. *The Origins of the Gothic Revival.* New Haven: Yale Univ. Press, 1987.

McClung, William Alexander. "The Architectonics of *Paradise Lost*." *VIA* 8 (1986): 33–39.

McCormick, Frank. *The Playwright as Architect.* University Park: Pennsylvania State Univ. Press, 1991.

Messer-Davidow, Ellen, David Shumway, and David J. Sylvan. Foreword to *The Recovery of Rhetoric: Persuasive Discourse and Disciplinarity in the Human Sciences.* Ed. R. H. Roberts and J. M. M. Good, x–xii. Charlottesville: Univ. Press of Virginia, 1993.

Milhous, Judith. *Thomas Betterton and the Management of Lincoln's Inn Fields, 1695–1708.* Carbondale: Southern Illinois Univ. Press, 1979.

Milhous, Judith, and Robert D. Hume. *Vice Chamberlain Coke's Theatrical Papers, 1706–1715.* Carbondale: Southern Illinois Univ. Press, 1982.

Millon, Henry. "The Architectural Theory of Francesco di Giorgio." *Art Bulletin* 40 (1958): 257–62.

Milton, John. *Complete Poems and Major Prose.* Ed. Merritt Y. Hughes. New York: Macmillan, 1957.

Mitchell, W. J. T. *Picture Theory: Essays on Verbal and Visual Representation.* Chicago: Univ. of Chicago Press, 1994.

Moretti, Franco. *Signs Taken for Wonders.* Rev. ed. New York: Verso, 1988.

Morris, Robert. *An Essay in Defense of Ancient Architecture; or, a Parallel of the Ancient Buildings with the Modern: shewing the Beauty and Harmony of the Former, and the Irregularity of the Latter. With Impartial Reflections on the Reasons of the Abuses Introduced by our Present Builders. To which is Annexed, An Inspectional TABLE,Universally Useful.* London, 1728.

———. *Rural architecture in the Gothick Taste.* London, 1750.

Mott, George. *Follies and Pleasure Pavilions: England, Ireland, Scotland, Wales.* New York: Harry N. Abrams, 1989.

Mowl, Timothy. *Horace Walpole: The Great Outsider*. London: John Murray, 1996.

Mowl, Timothy, and Brian Earnshaw. *Architecture without Kings: The Rise of Puritan Classicism under Cromwell*. New York: Manchester Univ. Press, 1995.

Moyles, R. G. *The Text of* Paradise Lost: *A Study in Editorial Procedure*. Toronto: Univ. of Toronto Press, 1985.

Nesbitt, Kate, ed. *Theorizing a New Agenda for Architecture: An Anthology of Architectural Theory, 1965–1995*. New York: Princeton Architectural Press, 1996

Nuttall, A. D. *Pope's "Essay on Man."* London: George Allen & Unwin, 1984.

Ockman, Joan, ed. *Architecture Culture, 1943–1968: A Documentary Anthology*. With the Collaboration of Edward Eigen. New York: Columbia Books of Architecture/Rizzoli, 1993.

Over, Charles. *Ornamental Architecture in the Gothic, Chinese and Modern Taste, being above fifty intire new designs of plans, sections, elevations, &c. (Many of which may be executed with roots of trees) for gardens, parks, forests, woods, canals, &c. Containing paling of several sorts, gates, garden seats, both close and open, Umbrello's, alcoves, grotto's, and grotesque seats, hermitages, triumphal arches, temples, banqueting houses and rooms, rotondo's, observatories, also, an obelisk or monument, with directions where proper to be erected, and the method how to execute them*. London, 1758.

Overton, Thomas Collins. *The Temple Builders Most Useful Companion, Being Fifty Entire New Original Designs for Pleasure and Recreation, consisting of Plans, Elevations, and Sections, in the Greek Roman and Gothic Taste: Calculated for the Ornamenting of Parks, Forests, Woods, Gardens, Canals, Eminences, Extensive Views, Mounts, Vistos, Islands, &c*. London, 1766.

Palladio, Andrea. *The First Book of Architecture. Translated out of the Italian With an Appendix Touching Doors and Windows By Pr. le Muet Translated out of French By G.R. [Geoffrey Richards]. To which are added Designs of Floors lately made at Somerset-House; And the Framing of Houses after the best manner of English Building with the Proportions and Scantlings*. London, 1663.

Pepys, Samuel. *The Shorter Pepys*. Ed. Robert Latham. Berkeley: Univ. of California Press, 1985.

Péréz Goméz, Alberto, and Louise Pelletier. *Architectural Representation and the Perspective Hinge*. Cambridge: MIT Press, 1997.

Perrault, Claude. *Ordonnance for the Five Kinds of Columns after the Method of the Ancients*. Trans. Indra Kagis McEwen. Santa Monica, CA: Getty Center for the History of Art and the Humanities, 1993.

Piano, Renzo. "The Building Workshop." In *Why Architects Draw*. Ed. Edward Robbins, 125–50. Cambridge: MIT Press, 1994.

Pigott, Stuart. *Ancient Britons and the Antiquarian Imagination: Ideas from the Renaissance to the Regency*. London: Thames and Hudson, 1989.

Pocock, J. G. A. *Virtue, Commerce, and History: Essays on Political Thought and History, Chiefly in the Eighteenth Century.* New York: Cambridge Univ. Press, 1985.

Pointon, Marcia R. *Milton and English Art.* Toronto: Univ. of Toronto Press, 1970.

Ponte, Allesandra. "Architecture and Phallocentrism in Richard Payne Knight's Theory." In *Sexuality and Space,* 273–305. Vol. 1 of *Princeton Papers on Architecture.* Ed. Beatriz Colomina. New York: Princeton Architectural Press, 1992.

Pope, Alexander. *The Correspondence of Alexander Pope.* Ed. George Sherburn. 4 vols. Oxford: Clarendon Press, 1956.

———. *The Poems of Alexander Pope.* Ed. John Butt. New Haven: Yale Univ. Press, 1963.

Porter, Roy. *London: A Social History.* Cambridge: Harvard Univ. Press, 1995.

Rawlins, Thomas. *Familiar Architecture, consisting of Original Designs of Houses for Gentlemen and Tradesmen, Patronages and Summer-Retreats, with Back-fronts, Sections, etc.* London, 1768.

Robbins, Edward. "The Social Uses of Drawing." In *Why Architects Draw,* 2–54. Ed. Edward Robbins. Cambridge: MIT Press, 1994.

Rogers, Pat. *Essays on Pope.* New York: Cambridge Univ. Press, 1993.

Roston, Murray. *Changing Perspectives in Literature and the Visual Arts, 1650–1820.* Princeton: Princeton Univ. Press, 1990.

Rouquet, André. *The Present State of the Arts in England.* 1755. Reprint, London: Cornmarket Press, 1970.

Rykwert, Joseph. *The Dancing Column.* Cambridge: MIT Press, 1996.

———. *The First Moderns: The Architects of the Eighteenth Century.* Cambridge: MIT Press, 1980.

———. *On Adam's House in Paradise: The Idea of the Primitive Hut in Architectural History.* 2d ed. Cambridge: MIT Press, 1981.

Sabor, Peter. *Horace Walpole: The Critical Heritage.* New York: Routledge, Kegan & Paul, 1987.

Schindler, Walter. *Voice and Crisis: Invocation in Milton's Poetry.* Hamdem, CT: Archon Books, 1984.

Scholes, Robert. *The Rise and Fall of English: Reconstructing English as a Discipline.* New Haven: Yale Univ. Press, 1998.

Schrag, Calvin O. *The Self after Postmodernity.* New Haven: Yale Univ. Press, 1997.

Seeley, Benton. *A Description of the Gardens of the Lord Viscount Cobham at Stow* (1744). Reprint, *Descriptions of Lord Cobham's Gardens at Stowe.* Ed. G. B. Clarke. 1744. Reprint, Dorchester, Dorset, UK: Buckinghamshire Record Society, 1990.

Shawcross, John T. "The Balanced Structure of *Paradise Lost.*" *Studies in Philology* 42:5 (Oct. 1965), 696–718.

Sitter, John. "The Flight from History in Mid-Eighteenth-Century Poetry (and Twentieth Century Criticism)." In *The Humanist as Citizen.* Ed. John Agresto and

Peter Riesenberg. Research Triangle Park, NC: National Humanities Center, 1981.

Sloterdijk, Peter. *Critique of Cynical Reason*. Trans. Michael Eldred. Minneapolis: Univ. of Minnesota Press, 1987.

Smith, Christine. *Architecture in the Culture of Early Humanism, 1400–1700*. New York: Oxford Univ. Press, 1992.

Snodin, Michael. *Horace Walpole and Strawberry Hill*. Richmond-upon-Thames: Orleans House Gallery, 1980.

Spence, Joseph. *Observations, Anecdotes, and Characters of Books and Men*. Ed. James M. Osborn. Oxford: Clarendon Press, 1966.

Sterne, Lawrence. *The Life and Opinions of Tristram Shandy*. Ed. Graham Petrie and Christopher Ricks. New York: Penguin, 1985.

Stukely, William. *Itinerarum Curiosum, or, an ACCOUNT of the ANTIQUITYS and remarkable CURIOSITYS in NATURE or ART, observ'd in Travels thro' GREAT BRITAIN. Illustrated with Copper Prints. CENTURIA I*. London, 1724.

———. *Stonehenge: A Temple Restor'd to the British Druids*. London, 1740.

Summerson, John. *Architecture in Britain, 1530–1830*. New York: Viking Penguin, 1986.

———. "The Classical Country House in 18th-Century England." *Journal of the Royal Society of Arts* 107:5036 (July 1959): 539–87.

———. *The Language of Classical Architecture*. Cambridge: MIT Press, 1963.

Swift, Jonathan. *The Complete Poems*. Ed. Pat Rogers. New Haven: Yale Univ. Press, 1983.

Tavernor, Robert. *Palladio and Palladianism*. New York: Thames & Hudson, 1991.

Tillotson, Geoffrey. *On the Poetry of Pope*. 2d ed. Oxford: Clarendon Press, 1950.

Thomas, David, ed. *Restoration and Georgian England, 1660–1788*. Cambridge Univ. Press, 1989.

Tschumi, Bernard. "Madness and the Combinative." *Precis* 5 (1984): 149–57.

Tzonis, Alexander, and Liane Lefaivre. *Classical Architecture: The Poetics of Order*. Cambridge: MIT Press, 1986.

Vanbrugh, Sir John. *The Complete Works*. 4 vols. Ed. Bonamy Dobrée and Geoffrey Webb. Bloomsbury: Nonesuch Press, 1927.

———. *The Provok'd Wife*. Ed. Curt A. Zimansky. Lincoln: Univ. of Nebraska Press, 1969.

———. *A Short Vindication of The Relapse and The Provok'd Wife from Immorality and Profaneness*. London, 1698.

Varey, Simon. *Space and the Eighteenth-Century Novel*. New York: Cambridge, 1990.

Venuti, Nicolo Marcello, marchesse de. *A description of the first discoveries of the ancient city of Herclea, found near Portici, a country palace belonging to the King of the Two Sicilies. In two parts*. London, 1750.

Vidler, Anthony. *The Architectural Uncanny: Essays in the Modern Unhomely*. Cambridge: MIT Press, 1992.

Vitruvius. *De architectura.* 2 vols. Trans. Frank Granger. Cambridge: Harvard Univ. Press, 1955.

Voltaire. *Letters on England.* Trans. Leonard Tancock. New York: Penguin, 1980.

———. *Philosophical Dictionary.* Trans. Theodore Besterman. New York: Penguin, 1972.

Walpole, Horace. *Anecdotes of Painting in England.* 1762–80. Reprint, New York: Arno Press, 1969.

———. *The Castle of Otranto.* Ed. W. S. Lewis. New York: Oxford Univ. Press, 1969.

———. *Correspondence.* Ed. W. S. Lewis. 50 vols. New Haven: Yale Univ. Press, 1937–83.

———. *A Description of the Villa of Mr. Horace Walpole, youngest son of Sir Robert Walpole Earl of Orford.* London, 1784.

Warburton, William. *A Vindication of Mr. Pope's* Essay on Man *from the misrepresentations of Mr De Crousaz, Professor of Philosophy and Mathematics in the Univ. of Lausanne. By the Author of* The Divine Legation of Moses Demonstrated. *In Six Letters.* 1725. Reprint, *The Eighteenth Century* 601, no. 21, Woodbridge, CT: Research Publications, 1985. Microfilm.

Webb, John. *A vindication of* Stone-Heng Restored: *in which the Orders and rules of Architecture Observed by the Ancient Romans, are discussed.* 2d ed. London, 1725.

Weber, Burton Jasper. *The Construction of* Paradise Lost. Carbondale: Southern Illinois Univ. Press, 1971.

Weinbrot, Howard D. "Gray's 'Progress of Poesy' and 'The Bard': An Essay in Literary Transmission." In *Johnson and His Age.* Ed. James Engell, 311–32. Cambridge: Harvard Univ. Press, 1984.

Whistler, Laurence. *The Imagination of Vanbrugh and His Fellow Artists.* London: Art and Technics, 1954.

———. *Sir John Vanbrugh: Architect and Dramatist, 1664–1726.* London: Cobden-Sanderson, 1938.

White, Hayden. *The Content of the Form: Narrative Discourse and Historical Representation.* Baltimore: Johns Hopkins Univ. Press, 1987.

Whitelaw, Jeffery W. *Follies.* Haverfordwest, UK: Shire Publications, 1982.

Wiebenson, Dora. "Documents of Social Change: Publications about the Small House." In *Studies in Eighteenth-Century British Art and Aesthetics.* Ed. Ralph Cohen. Berkeley: Univ. of California Press, 1985.

Wilton-Ely, John. "The Rise of the Professional Architect." In *The Architect: Chapters in the History of the Profession.* Ed. Spiro Kostof. Oxford: Oxford Univ. Press, 1977.

Wittkower, Rudolf. *Architectural Principles in the Age of Humanism.* New York: W. W. Norton & Co., 1971.

———. *Palladio and English Palladianism.* New York: Thames and Hudson, 1983.

Wood, John. *Choir Gaure vulgarly called Stonehenge . . . Described, Restored, and explained.* Oxford, 1747.

———. *The Origin of Building: or, the Plagiarism of the Heathen Detected.* Bath, 1741.

Worsley, Giles. *Classical Architecture in Britain: The Heroic Age.* New Haven: Yale Univ. Press, 1995.

———. "Wicked Woman of Marl." *Country Life* 185:11 (14 March 1991): 44–47.

Wotton, Sir Henry. *The Elements of Architecture. A Facsimile Reprint of the First Edition.* 1624. Reprint, Charlottesville: Univ. Press of Virginia, 1968.

Wrighte, William. *Grotesque Architecture, or Rural Amusement; consisting of Plans, Elevations and Sections, for Huts, Retreats, Summer and Winter Hermitages, Terminaries, Chinese, Gothic and Natural Grottos, Cascades, Baths, Mosques, Moresque Pavilions, Grotesque and Rustic Seats, Green Houses, &c.* London, 1790.

Zimbardo, Rose A. *A Mirror to Nature: Transformations in Drama and Aesthetics, 1660–1732.* Lexington: Univ. Press of Kentucky, 1986.

Index